The Kitchen
Companion

Photography
Cut-out photographs: Paul Turner and Sue Pressley
Recipe photographs: Peter Barry

Design
Paul Turner and Sue Pressley, Stonecastle Graphics Ltd

Editorial
Compiled by Wendy Hobson
Edited by Dana Holmes

Production
Ruth Arthur
Sally Connolly
Neil Randles

Director of Production
Gerald Hughes

CLB 3191
© 1992 CLB Publishing, Godalming, Surrey
All rights reserved
This 1993 edition published by Crescent Books,
distributed by Outlet Book Company, Inc.,
a Random House Company
40 Engelhard Avenue, Avenel, New Jersey 07001

Random House
New York • Toronto • London • Sydney • Auckland

Printed and bound in Italy
ISBN 0 517 08771 5
8 7 6 5 4 3 2 1

The Kitchen
Companion

Your Seasonal Guide to Delicious Recipes

Compiled and edited by Wendy Hobson

CRESCENT BOOKS
NEW YORK • AVENEL, NEW JERSEY

Making the Most of the Seasons

Every SEASON and every month of the year has its own special associations: from the rich and warming soups that ward off the cold of a January day to the luscious soft fruits of summer, the crisp red apples of fall, and all the traditional delights of the Christmas season.

The Kitchen Companion contains a seasonal selection of recipes, hints and tips to help you make the best of foods in season and create tasty dishes every month of the year. Of course, you do not have to restrict yourself to making the dishes at one particular time of the year, for you are sure to find favorites you will want to cook again and again.

Many foods are now available in the supermarket throughout the year, and are often of excellent quality, even when out of season. But they can be more expensive then, so consider both price and quality. It is often the best idea to use foods when they are in season, particularly fruits and vegetables. Not only are they cheapest at that time, but the flavor will be at its best. You may be able to buy beautiful Brussels sprouts in March, but the taste could be bitter and will not compare with the sweet, nutty sprouts you can buy at Christmas. Tomatoes are available throughout the year, but you will find that the tastiest, juiciest ones are those that have ripened under a summer sun. And with every month offering you a different selection of produce, there is always something to look forward to.

Try to use fresh produce whenever possible. It will not only taste best, but is also the best for you, for it will contain its full complement of vitamins and minerals. Avoid buying foods that look faded or tired; they are past their prime.

If you are short of time to prepare fresh foods or want to use produce out of season, look for canned or frozen varieties, many of which offer excellent value and quality. Keep basic ingredients on hand so you can always put together something interesting at short notice.

Many of the recipes in this book are simple and quick to prepare, so they are ideal for the busy household where you need a tasty and nutritious meal without complicated preparation or long cooking times.

All of the recipes are simply presented so you can see at a glance what you need and how to prepare it. There are many suggestions for variations to recipes, and you can always experiment to make your own versions of the dishes. If you do not have a particular ingredient, just look through the recipe and see whether you can leave it out, or if you can substitute something else you have on hand. Never be afraid to try out new ideas of your own, especially using foods you have grown yourself, and those that are in season or are readily available.

You will not need any special kitchen equipment. Of course, if you have a food processor, blender or mixer, use them to speed up slicing, chopping, blending or any other preparation.

Cooking Tips

THESE HANDY tips will help you to make the best of your *Kitchen Companion*.

1 Store foods carefully to maintain their freshness. Always remove plastic wrappings, because they will cause foods to sweat. Store fruits and vegetables on a cool shelf or at the bottom of the refrigerator. Wrap cheese or cooked meats in aluminum foil and store in the refrigerator, removing cheese 1 hour before serving to allow it to ripen. Place raw meats on a plate, cover well and make sure they do not come into contact with other foods in the refrigerator.

2 Note expiration dates when you are shopping and use up fresh foods by the date indicated.

3 Always wash fresh produce before preparation.

4 Use large eggs. If you do not have them simply add a little more or less liquid to the mixture to obtain the correct consistency.

5 Spoon measurements are level. It is best to use a set of measuring spoons; spoons intended for serving food vary in size according to the design.

6 Adjust seasoning and strongly-flavored ingredients such as onions and garlic according to your own taste. If you do not care for a particularly strong spice or flavoring, leave it out or substitute something else.

7 Use fresh herbs where possible, because they will give you the best flavor and texture. There are only a few exceptions, such as oregano, the flavor of which develops when it is properly dried. If you do substitute dried for fresh herbs, use only half the amount specified but do not use dried herbs for garnish or adding at the end of a recipe or they will taste raw.

8 Always use freshly ground black pepper for seasoning. If you do not use salt in your cooking, you may wish to add a few additional herbs.

9 For convenience, the recipes list "butter," but you can substitute margarine if you prefer.

10 If you do not have the cookware indicated in the recipe, look at the photograph and select the most suitable item you have.

11 Because ovens vary, cooking times and temperatures are approximate and may need to be adjusted to suit your oven. Convection ovens, for example, will need lower temperatures and the food will take less time to cook. You know your own oven best so adjust times and temperatures as necessary.

12 All the recipes serve 4 unless otherwise indicated.

Kitchen Cupboard

A WELL-STOCKED cupboard means you can always prepare a simple but tasty meal at those times when you need to put together something from nothing! Use these suggestions to give you more ideas.

Bottles and jars: honey, jam, oil, corn syrup, molasses.
Cans: lentils, peas and beans, corned beef, fruits in natural juice, salmon, tuna.
Dry goods: baking powder, baking soda, baking chocolate, flour, oatmeal, pasta, rice, ladyfingers or cookies, chicken and beef stock cubes, sugar.
Frozen goods: phyllo dough, fish fillets, shrimp, puff pastry.
Fruits and nuts: almonds, ground almonds, dried fruits, walnuts.

Herbs and spices: cayenne pepper, cinnamon, curry powder, nutmeg, oregano, mixed herbs, parsley, pepper, salt.
Miscellaneous: butter, eggs, chocolate, gelatin, evaporated milk.
Sauces: tomato paste, Worcestershire sauce, soy sauce.
Vegetables: carrots, onions, potatoes.
Bean Salad: Drain, rinse and mix a selection of canned beans. Top with French dressing (see page iv) and sprinkle with fresh herbs.

Fish Sticks: Coat strips of fish fillet in egg and flour and fry in butter or oil. Serve with a white sauce (see page iv) flavored with chopped fresh parsley, potatoes and peas.

Shrimp Twists: Make a thick white sauce (see page iv) using half milk and half chicken stock and stir in some shrimp. Use to fill little bundles made of layers of phyllo dough brushed with oil and twisted together at the top. Brush with oil and bake in a preheated oven at 400°F for 10 minutes.

Corned Beef Fritters: Coat cubes of corned beef in a thick batter (see page iv) and fry until golden.

Tuna Pie: Line a pie plate with shortcrust pastry (see page iv), spread with drained tuna and season with salt, pepper and cayenne pepper. Beat 2 eggs with ⅔ cup cream or milk, pour over the tuna and bake in a preheated oven at 400°F for 30 minutes.

Pasta Bowl: Mix cooked pasta with a selection of beans, chopped onion, shrimp, or chopped corned beef. Mix with mayonnaise (see page iv) flavored with tomato paste or curry powder.

Angel Dessert: Layer ladyfingers or cake and drained canned fruit in a bowl and use the juice to make a jello. Spoon the jello over the fruit and leave to set. Top with custard and decorate with grated chocolate.

Chocolate Cake: Beat together ⅔ cup milk, ⅔ cup corn oil, 2 eggs, 2 tablespoons corn syrup, 1⅓ cups flour, ⅔ cup sugar, 2 tablespoons baking chocolate, 1 teaspoon baking soda, 1 teaspoon baking powder. Bake in 2 greased and floured 8-inch cake pans for 35 minutes. Sandwich together with whipped cream.

Basic Recipes

Stock

1 chicken carcass,	1 onion
meat bones or fish heads,	1 carrot
bones and skin	1 stalk celery

Place the meat or fish in a saucepan with a selection of vegetables to give the stock flavor. Cover with cold water, bring slowly to a boil and simmer for 1½ hours. Strain, then return the stock to the pan and boil to reduce the liquid. Use immediately or freeze.

Batter

⅔ cup flour	1 egg
Pinch of salt	⅔ cup milk

Beat all the ingredients together until the batter is smooth. Alter the amount of milk to adjust the consistency of the batter.

White Sauce

2 tablespoons butter	1¼ cups milk
¼ cup flour	

Melt the butter, stir in the flour and cook for 1 minute. Whisk in the milk and bring to a boil, stirring continuously until the sauce thickens. Alter the amount of milk used to thicken or thin the sauce.

French Dressing

8 tablespoons salad oil
4 tablespoons wine vinegar
2 teaspoons Dijon mustard
Salt and pepper

Shake all the ingredients together well in a screw-top jar.

Mayonnaise

1 egg	2 tablespoons lemon juice
1 egg yolk	1 tablespoon white wine vinegar
½ teaspoon salt	1⅔ cups oil
½ teaspoon dry mustard	

Place all the ingredients except the oil in a blender and mix well. Add one-third of the oil and mix again. With the blender running, gradually pour in the remaining oil until the mayonnaise thickens. Add spices, herbs or tomato paste if desired.

Basic Bread

8 cups flour	2 tablespoons solid shortening
2 tablespoons salt	3¾ cups warm water
1 tablespoon active dry yeast	

Mix together the flour, salt, shortening and dry yeast in a food processor. Keep processor on and gradually add water until the mixture forms a dough. Process until smooth and elastic and no longer sticky. Cover and leave to rise for 2 hours. Knead again, place in greased loaf pans, cover and leave to rise for 1 hour more. Bake in a 450°F oven for 40 minutes.

Shortcrust Pastry

1⅓ cups flour	4 tablespoons solid shortening
Pinch of salt	3 tablespoons water
4 tablespoons butter	

Sift the flour and salt. Mix in the butter and shortening until the mixture resembles bread crumbs. Add enough water to make a soft pastry. Handle the dough as little as possible. Use as directed in the recipe.

Cooking for Children

MOST CHILDREN love cooking, and they can have lots of fun in a well-supervised kitchen making meals for their family and friends. Always remember that safety comes first. Teach children to be careful of sharp knives and graters, hot pans, food, foil, ovens and steam. Always supervise children while they are cooking.

Sausage Casserole

1 pound bulk sausage
2 tablespoons flour
Salt and pepper
1 cooking apple, peeled, cored and sliced

1 onion, sliced
½ teaspoon dried mixed herbs
14 ounces canned tomatoes

Heat oven to 350°F. Divide the sausage into 16 equal balls. Sprinkle the flour with salt and pepper and roll the balls in the flour. Place the apple, onion and sausage balls in an ovenproof dish. Sprinkle with herbs and pour tomatoes over mixture. Sprinkle with salt and pepper. Cover and cook for 1 hour. Serve with mashed potatoes and peas.

Baked Cheese Fingers

8 large slices brown bread
2 tablespoons butter
4 slices cheese

1 egg, beaten
⅔ cup milk
Salt and pepper

Heat oven to 350°F. Remove crusts from the bread and butter each slice. Put cheese on 4 slices of bread and cover with remaining slices. Cut each sandwich into 3 fingers. Mix the egg and milk and sprinkle with salt and pepper. Dip the sandwiches into the milk mixture and arrange in a shallow ovenproof dish. Pour on any remaining mixture. Bake for 15 minutes. Serve with salad.

Potato Surprises

4 baking potatoes, scrubbed
2 tablespoons butter
2 tablespoons milk

⅔ cup grated cheese
4 eggs

Heat oven to 400°F. Cut a cross through the skins of the potatoes and bake for 1 hour until soft. Allow to cool. Scoop the potato into a bowl and mash with the butter, milk and cheese. Fill each potato skin half full with the cheese mixture. Break an egg into each one. Cover with the remaining cheese mixture and brown under the broiler.

Hot Ham Crusties

4 dinner rolls
6 tablespoons soft margarine
Grated peel of ½ orange

1 teaspoon chopped fresh parsley
⅔ cup ham, chopped
Salt and pepper

Heat oven to 375°F. Cut a thin slice off the top of each roll. Pull out the centers and crumble into bread crumbs. Mix bread crumbs with other ingredients and spoon back into rolls. Replace the tops and wrap each one in aluminum foil. Place on a baking sheet and bake for 20 minutes. Serve hot.

Pudding Pie

10 gingersnaps
4 tablespoons butter
1 large banana
1 package instant butterscotch pudding
2 cups milk
1 chocolate bar

Place the gingersnaps in a bag and crush them with a rolling pin. Melt the butter in a saucepan. Remove from the heat and mix in the gingersnap crumbs. Press the mixture into the base of a pie plate and leave to cool and set. Slice the banana and arrange the slices on the crumb base. Prepare the pudding mix with the milk according to the instructions on the package. Pour over the banana and allow to set. Decorate with chocolate shavings.

Fairy Cupcakes

1 cup soft margarine
½ cup sugar
⅔ cup flour
1 teaspoon baking powder
2 eggs
1¼ cups powdered sugar
24 M&Ms

Heat oven to 350°F. Mix together ⅔ cup margarine with the sugar, flour, baking powder and eggs until smooth and soft. Spoon the mixture into paper baking cups in a cupcake pan and bake for about 15 minutes. Allow cakes to cool. Place the remaining margarine in a bowl and sift in the powdered sugar. Mix together to make icing. You can add a few drops of food coloring if you wish. Spread some icing on each cake and top with an M&M.

January

"Silent and soft and slow
Descends the snow"

Henry Wadsworth Longfellow

CHRISTMAS is over and the
New Year begins with resolutions – which may even be
kept! Heavy snows blanket the world outdoors, but
inside, the kitchen offers the comfort of rich and
nourishing soups and stews, flavored with a spoonful of
sherry or wine. The best meals for these frigid days are
filling and satisfying, the perfect way of banishing winter
chills. Days are short now and the long evenings are best
spent enjoying the coziness of home.

JANUARY

1 New Year's Day

2 Resolve to try some different cheese this year: German Tilsit and Spanish Valgrande are especially delicious.

3

4 Select unblemished oranges for marmalade. Squeeze the juice from 3 pounds of oranges and 2 lemons. Tie the seeds in cheesecloth. Soak the chopped peel overnight in 4½ quarts water. Add the seeds and juice and simmer for 1½ hours until the peel is soft. Discard the seeds, stir in 12 cups sugar and boil for 20 minutes until set.

5 To make a wintertime vegetable soup, combine chicken stock with your favorite vegetables, blend into a purée and stir in a spoonful of light cream.

6

7

Onion Soup

2 pounds onions, sliced
2 teaspoons sugar
4 tablespoons margarine
⅓ cup flour
7½ cups chicken or
   vegetable stock
⅔ cup dry white wine

1 teaspoon dried thyme
Salt and pepper
12 slices French bread
2 tablespoons olive oil
⅓ cup grated Cheddar
   cheese
Fresh parsley for garnish

Brown onions and sugar in margarine for 15 minutes, stirring occasionally. Stir in the flour and cook for 1 minute. Gradually stir in the stock, wine, salt and pepper. Partially cover and simmer for 30 minutes.

Lightly brush both sides of the bread slices with oil and broil one side until pale golden. Turn the bread over, sprinkle with the cheese and broil until golden brown. Serve the soup in individual bowls with the bread slices floating on top. Garnish with fresh parsley.

Brushing the bread with olive oil makes it delightfully crisp when toasted under a hot broiler, giving a good contrast to the smooth soup. Try any hard cheese of your choice for the croutons: Gruyère or Parmesan impart pleasantly strong flavors.

8

9

For Duchess Potatoes, beat 1 egg into mashed potatoes, force through pastry tube to make swirls and bake at 400°F for 30 minutes.

10

11

12

Lay pork chops on a bed of sliced apples, onions and mushrooms, pour on some apple juice, top with bread crumbs and cheese and bake for 40 minutes.

13

14

To make apple wings as a garnish, cut an apple in half and lay it cut side down. Make 2 diagonal cuts and lift out a small wedge from the top. Continue to cut, following the lines of the first cut, until 2 wedges remain. Reshape the apple and gently separate the slices to form a wing shape.

Marinated Pork

4 pork chops
1 onion, finely chopped
½ teaspoon dried sage
½ teaspoon dried thyme
1 cup hard cider
2 tablespoons oil
1 tablespoon butter

⅔ cup flour
Salt and pepper
2 apples, peeled, cored and
  sliced
¾ cup chicken stock
1 teaspoon honey
1 teaspoon Dijon mustard

Marinate the chops with the onion, herbs and cider for at least 2 hours, turning occasionally.

Heat oven to 350° F. Drain chops and strain the marinade. Heat oil and butter in large skillet. Season flour with salt and pepper and lightly dust chops; set aside remaining flour. Brown chops in skillet. Spread apples in a greased cooking dish and place chops on top. Fry the strained onions for 5 minutes until soft. Stir in remaining flour, brown lightly, then stir in marinade, stock, honey and mustard. Bring to a boil and pour over chops. Cover and cook for 45 minutes. Serve with creamed potatoes and peas.

Marinating meat or fish in oil, cider or wine before cooking tenderizes it, while the herbs give it extra flavor. Cover the meat and leave it in a cool place for at least 2 hours or overnight if possible.

JANUARY

15

16

To save time, use canned beans, draining and rinsing them well before adding them to the pan.

17

18

19

Use peas, beans or lentils as vegetables with broiled meats to provide healthy and colorful side dishes.

20

21

All beans should be soaked overnight in cold water, then drained and rinsed thoroughly. To cook them, cover with fresh water, bring to a full boil and simmer for about 1 hour until tender. Red kidney beans must be boiled for 15 minutes before simmering to destroy any toxins they contain.

Quick Goulash

1 onion, finely chopped
1 clove garlic, crushed
1 carrot, diced
2 zucchini, diced
2 tablespoons olive oil
1 tablespoon paprika
Pinch of freshly grated
  nutmeg
2 tablespoons chopped fresh
  parsley

1 tablespoon tomato paste
14 ounces canned
  tomatoes
8 ounces cooked kidney
  beans
⅔ cup tomato juice
Salt and pepper
2 tablespoons sour cream or
  plain yogurt

Fry the onion, garlic, carrot and zucchini in the oil for 5 minutes until soft. Stir in the paprika, nutmeg, parsley and tomato paste and cook for 1 minute. Stir in the tomatoes, beans, tomato juice, salt and pepper. Cover and cook for 15 minutes. Transfer to a warm serving dish and drizzle the cream or yogurt over the top. Serve with warm crusty bread and a salad of watercress and cabbage.

You can choose almost any type of beans for this dish: black-eyed peas, navy beans, soy beans or pinto beans. The recipe also tastes good with chick peas or lentils. Use a selection to give a variety of tastes and a wonderful range of colors.

JANUARY

22

For a moist result, simmer chicken half covered in water or stock with a few vegetables for about 1½ hours.

26

23

27

Fill tiny bottled peppers with a stuffing of ground meats and herbs and deep-fry for a delicious hot appetizer or snack.

24

28

25

You can also make Shrimp or Crab Nuggets with finely chopped shrimp or crab claws instead of chicken. Leave out the chili if you prefer a milder flavor, or substitute ¼ of a finely chopped green or red pepper.

Chicken Nuggets

2⅔ cups cooked chicken, minced
¾ cup bread crumbs
2 tablespoons butter
2 tablespoons flour
⅔ cup milk
2 eggs, beaten

½ red or green chili, seeded and chopped
1 green onion, chopped
1 tablespoon chopped fresh parsley
Salt and pepper
Oil for deep-frying

You can either dip the chicken balls into the egg and turn with a fork, or brush them lightly with the egg using a pastry brush. If you pressed the ingredients together well when you combined them, they should not break up.

Mix together the chicken and half of the bread crumbs. Melt the butter, stir in half of the flour and cook for 1 minute. Gradually stir in the milk and bring to a boil to make a thick white sauce. Stir in the chicken and bread crumbs with the chili, onion, parsley, salt and pepper, and allow to cool.

Dust hands with flour and shape mixture into 1-inch balls. Coat with beaten egg and roll in bread crumbs. Deep-fry in hot oil for about 5 minutes until golden brown. Drain on paper towels and sprinkle lightly with salt before serving.

Nuggets made with chicken or fish can be served cold as a party snack, or hot with French fries and baked beans for dinner.

JANUARY

29

30

31

Make sure you wash leeks thoroughly before slicing to remove any grit lodged between the layers.

Use whatever shellfish you prefer for this recipe, but make sure you buy them fresh and use them quickly. Whatever you choose – clams, mussels, scallops – scrub them well and soak them in several changes of fresh water. Discard any that do not close when tapped or do not open during cooking.

If you buy live lobster, cook it with the other shellfish until it turns red, then remove and prepare it. Otherwise, use cooked lobster, fresh or frozen. Cut it in half lengthwise, cut off the tail and remove the meat. Crack the claws and remove the meat as whole as possible. Discard the head. Buy raw shrimp, if possible, for the sweetest flavor, but cooked shrimp will also taste delicious.

Fish Stock

1 pound fish bones, skin and heads
8 cups water
1 onion, sliced
1 carrot, sliced
1 bay leaf
6 black peppercorns
Pinch of ground mace
1 sprig fresh thyme or 1 tsp dried
1 slice lemon

Bring all the stock ingredients to a boil, simmer for 20 minutes. Strain the stock and discard the fish and vegetables.

Bouillabaisse

1 carrot, sliced
2 leeks, sliced
1 clove garlic, crushed
⅓ cup butter
Pinch of saffron
½ cup dry white wine
1 cup canned tomatoes
1 pound cod or halibut fillets
1 pound mussels, scrubbed
1 pound small clams, scrubbed
8 small new potatoes, scrubbed
1 lobster, prepared
8 ounces large peeled shrimp
1 tablespoon chopped fresh parsley

Fry carrot, leeks and garlic in butter for 5 minutes until soft. Add saffron and wine and simmer for 5 minutes. Add stock and remaining ingredients except the lobster, shrimp and parsley. Bring to a boil and simmer for about 15 minutes until the shellfish have opened and the potatoes are tender. Add lobster and shrimp, remove from heat, cover and allow to stand for 5 minutes. Sprinkle with parsley and serve with garlic bread and a glass of lightly chilled dry white wine.

February

"The Summer hath his joys,
And Winter his delights.
Though Love and all his pleasures are but toys,
They shorten tedious nights."

Thomas Campion

SPRING still seems months aways in the dark days of February – leaden skies can make the shortest month feel like the longest. Brighten these times with a vegetable curry and other warming dish. Whimsical nature sometimes gives the gift of a winter thaw, melting off the snow and encouraging hardy crocuses to peep out, but all too often they'll have to duck their heads as winter returns. One bright spot this month is Valentine's Day, when you can let the romantic in you run wild!

FEBRUARY

1

2

3 Chinese shrimp crackers, fried briefly in hot oil, make a good side dish for a Chinese meal or a tasty cocktail snack.

4

5 Finish a Chinese meal with a glass of jasmine tea, which is available in most supermarkets.

6

7

Remove the hard central core from the tomatoes with a sharp knife and cut them into wedges. Wait until the last minute to add them to the wok, so they retain their shape and a slight crispness. Snowpeas or mushrooms also go well with this sauce, with or without peppers.

Cantonese Beef

4 tablespoons soy sauce
1 tablespoon cornstarch
1 tablespoon dry sherry
1 teaspoon sugar
1 pound rump steak, cut
   into thin strips
2 large tomatoes, cut into
   wedges

2 tablespoons salted black
   beans
2 tablespoons water
4 tablespoons vegetable oil
1 green pepper, cut into
   chunks
¾ cup beef stock
Pepper

Look for salted black beans in specialty food shops. Crush the beans in a small bowl with the back of a spoon to make a thick paste – this gives a truly authentic flavor.

Mix together the soy sauce, cornstarch, sherry and sugar. Add the meat and set aside. Core the tomatoes and cut them into wedges. Add water to beans and crush them to a paste. Heat the oil in a wok and stir-fry the pepper for 2 minutes, then remove. Add the meat and marinade and stir-fry for 2 minutes. Add the bean paste and stock, bring to a boil and simmer for 5 minutes until slightly thickened. Add the pepper and tomatoes, season and stir-fry for 1 minute. Serve immediately with boiled rice.

FEBRUARY

8

12

9

13

Fold puréed canned peaches into whipped cream with a touch of cinnamon, chill and serve with gingersnaps.

10

Wash and dry some rose petals. Dip in whisked egg whites and then sugar, allow to dry and use to decorate special desserts.

14 **Valentine's Day**

11

To make the raspberry sauce, purée 1 cup fresh or frozen raspberries then rub them through a sieve to remove the seeds. Stir in 2½ tablespoons powdered sugar to sweeten. This is delicious with the Valentine Creams, poured over ice cream or swirled into yogurt.

Valentine Creams

8 ounces cream cheese
1¾ cups heavy cream

⅔ cup powdered sugar
2 teaspoons ground cinnamon

Whisk the cream cheese with 4 tablespoons of cream until light and fluffy. Sift in the powdered sugar and cinnamon and blend well. Whip the remaining cream until stiff and fold it into the mixture. Line 4 molds with damp cheesecloth, spoon in the cream and press down to remove any air bubbles. Fold the cheesecloth over the top and stand molds on a rack with a tray underneath. Refrigerate for at least 8 hours. Turn out carefully, spoon some raspberry sauce over each and serve garnished with candied rose petals.

Use molds with small holes in the bottom so any excess liquid can drain away during chilling. Line the molds with damp cheesecloth, extending the material beyond the edges of the molds.

FEBRUARY

15

16

17

An onion and tomato salad tastes good with Indian foods. Finely slice onions and mix with thin tomato wedges.

18

Spices are used in Indian foods to benefit the digestion as well as to provide flavor and color. Cook them before adding other ingredients to avoid a harsh taste. Peel ginger root before grating; do not use ground ginger. Wash your hands after preparing chilies because they contain an irritant.

19

20

If you have time, prepare and cook curries in advance and reheat them; because this improves the flavor.

21

Vegetable Curry

1 onion, finely chopped
1 green chili pepper, seeded
   and finely chopped
1 small piece ginger root,
   grated

14 ounces canned
   tomatoes, drained
2 cups cauliflower florets
⅔ cup vegetable stock
½ pound okra

2 cloves garlic, crushed
1 tablespoon oil
½ teaspoon ground cumin
½ teaspoon ground turmeric
2 potatoes, diced
1 eggplant, cubed

4 ounces roasted, unsalted
   cashew nuts
6 tablespoons flaked coconut
Salt and pepper
4 tablespoons plain yogurt

Fry onion, chili, ginger and garlic in oil for 5 minutes until soft. Stir in spices and fry for 1 minute. Stir in potatoes, eggplant and tomatoes. Cover and cook for 10 minutes until the vegetables are almost tender. Add the cauliflower, stock and okra, cover and cook for 5 minutes until the vegetables are tender. Add the cashews, coconut, salt and pepper, heat through, then transfer to a warm serving dish. Drizzle the yogurt over the top and serve with pilau rice.

Use any of your favorite vegetables for this delicious curry. Try sliced zucchini, peas, carrots or broccoli.
Remember to first add those vegetables that cook longest so they all finish cooking at the same time.

FEBRUARY

22

Basil has a strong flavor, so don't use too much. If you do not have fresh basil, stir in a little pesto sauce.

26

23

27

Most of the fat in chicken is contained in the skin, so remove it before or after cooking for a healthier meal.

24

28/29

25

Use a very sharp knife to peel limes, lemons or oranges so you remove all of the white membrane, which can be bitter. Remove the fibrous center and push out any seeds. Slice as thinly as possible, retaining the shape of the fruit.

Lime-Roasted Chicken

4 chicken breasts
Salt and pepper
4 limes
2 teaspoons white wine
  vinegar

5 tablespoons olive oil
2 teaspoons chopped
  fresh basil
1 sprig fresh basil

Rub chicken with salt and pepper, place in an ovenproof dish and set aside. Pare away thin strips of peel from 2 limes, then cut them in half and squeeze the juice. Mix the lime juice and rind with the wine vinegar and 4 tablespoons of oil, pour over the chicken, cover and refrigerate for at least 4 hours – overnight if possible – basting occasionally.

Heat oven to 375° F. Baste the chicken then bake for 30 minutes until tender. Meanwhile, peel and slice the remaining limes. Heat remaining oil and fry lime slices and basil for 1 minute until they begin to soften. Arrange the chicken on a warm serving platter, pour on the sauce and garnish with the basil sprig. Serve with creamed potatoes and steamed snowpeas lightly tossed in butter.

Vary the recipe by using lemons and thyme instead of lime and basil for a slightly sharper taste. Always make sure chicken is thoroughly cooked by spearing the thickest point with a skewer. If the juices run clear, the chicken is ready.

March

"When daffodils begin to peer,
With heigh! the doxy, over the dale,
Why, then comes in the sweet o' the year;
For the red blood reigns in the winter's pale."

William Shakespeare

THE winds may still be strong and the rains frequent, but occasionally a day breaks out in glorious sunshine, a reminder of the promise of spring. The first flowers push through the cold earth. Suggestions of nature's coming bounty, whether home grown or bought, stir ideas in every cook's mind. New life is breathing in the kitchen, too, with the new vegetables of the season, crisp and tender, ready for lighter dishes to come.

MARCH

1 Leeks are a special springtime treat. Slice them into rings, fry them in a little butter and chicken stock and serve with lamb chops.

2

3

4

5

6 Make Breton pancakes with buckwheat flour and serve them with a ham and cheese filling and a mug of hard cider.

7 Pancakes can be filled with almost anything you like, then rolled up and baked or simply served as they are to create a perfect snack, lunch or dessert. Try cottage cheese and walnuts, mushrooms in sauce, shrimp, cooked smoked haddock with chopped tomato and onion, cherries with yogurt.

French Pancakes

⅔ cup flour
Pinch of salt
1 egg, beaten
1¼ cups milk
1 tablespoon vegetable oil

Juice and pared peel
of 1 lemon
Juice and pared peel
of 1 orange

Mix flour and salt and make a well in the center. Beat egg and milk and stir it into the flour, then beat to a smooth batter. Heat a little oil in a pancake pan and pour on some batter, tilting the pan so the batter spreads as thinly as possible. Cook on one side, toss or turn with a spatula and brown the other side. Layer pancakes between sheets of parchment paper and keep them warm while you fry the remaining batter. Garnish with citrus peel and serve with the juice.

The best way to pare thin strips from citrus fruits is to use a lemon zester. Otherwise use a very sharp knife and cut the peel into strips. Make sure you cut off any white membrane since this tastes bitter.

MARCH

8

9

Mix poached, flaked sole with shrimp, chopped hard-boiled eggs, parsley and white sauce. Top with mashed potatoes and bake.

10

11

12

13

14

Try making turnovers with meat, chicken or vegetables for a lunch box or a picnic on a warm spring day.

You can make mushroom turnovers with 1½ cups mushrooms and 4 tablespoons bread crumbs stirred into a white sauce made with 2 tablespoons butter, 3 tablespoons flour and ½ cup each milk and vegetable stock.

Sole Turnovers

4 sole fillets, skinned
Salt and pepper
6 tablespoons milk
⅔ cup small mushrooms,
  sliced
2 tablespoons butter
Juice of 1 lemon

3 tablespoons coarsely
  ground hazelnuts
12 ounces frozen puff
  pastry
1 egg, beaten
1 teaspoon poppy seeds

Heat oven to 350° F. Season fish with salt and pepper, roll up
and secure with wooden picks. Place in ovenproof dish with
milk; cover and cook in oven for 10 minutes. Drain, remove
picks and allow to cool. Cook mushrooms, butter and lemon
juice in a small saucepan for about 5 minutes. Cool, then stir
in hazelnuts. Roll out pastry and cut into 4 circles, 6 inches
each. Place a fish roll on each and divide stuffing mixture
among them. Brush edges with beaten egg and pinch
together to seal. Brush all over with egg and sprinkle with
poppy seeds. Raise oven temperature to 400° F. Bake until
puffed and golden. Serve with a green salad and potatoes
glazed in butter.

To seal a turnover, make
sure you have brushed the
edges well with beaten egg.
Pull the pastry edges up and
over the filling and pinch the
edges together firmly. You
may want to try using a
pastry press.

MARCH

15

Smother slices of flank steak with sliced onions and a little stock, cover and cook in a low oven for 2 hours.

19

16

20

Grind 1½ pounds steak and mix with 1 egg, ½ cup bread crumbs, 1 chopped onion and seasoning to make tasty meatballs.

17 **St. Patrick's Day**

21

18

For Irish Griddle Scones, knead ⅔ cup self-rising flour, ½ teaspoon salt, 3 tablespoons butter, ½ teaspoon freshly grated nutmeg, 1 egg and 6 tablespoons milk. Make 2 circles ½ inch thick, cut into 6 triangles; cook on greased griddle for 5 minutes each side.

Traditionally a drink to accompany oysters fresh from the sea, Guinness is synonymous with Ireland, and they say that nowhere but in Ireland does it taste exactly as it should. It gives a wonderful rich flavor and tenderizes meat during the long slow cooking.

Beef in Guinness

1½ pounds chuck steak
½ pound carrots
3 tablespoons vegetable oil
2 onions, chopped
3 tablespoons flour
Salt and pepper

½ teaspoon chopped fresh
* basil or ¼ tsp dried*
⅔ cup Guinness or ale
1 teaspoon honey
⅔ cup beef stock

Heat oven to 325° F. Cut steak into 12 pieces 1 inch thick. Trim carrots into 2½-inch pieces. Heat oil in a skillet and fry onions until soft; use a slotted spoon to transfer them to a shallow, greased ovenproof dish. Season flour, dip in the meat and fry in oil until browned, then transfer to casserole with the carrots. Stir flour in the skillet and cook for 1 minute. Stir in basil and Guinness, bring to a boil and simmer for 1 minute. Stir in honey and stock, return to a boil and pour over the meat. Cover and bake for 1½ hours. Serve with mashed or boiled potatoes and lightly steamed cabbage.

MARCH

22

Dip onion rings into a thick flour and water batter, fry until crisp and serve with broiled meat and ratatouille.

26

23

27

24

Garlic is very popular in European cooking. It gives a wonderful flavor and is also very good for you.

28

25

Eggplant contains bitter juices that must be extracted before you use them. Cut eggplant in half or in thick slices and make diagonal cuts on the exposed sides. Sprinkle with salt and place them in a colander so the juices can drain off. Rinse well under running water and pat dry before use.

Ratatouille

2 eggplants
Salt
4 tablespoons olive oil
2 Spanish onions, thinly
  sliced
4 zucchini, sliced
1 red pepper, chopped

1 green pepper, chopped
2 tablespoons chopped fresh
  basil or 1 tablespoon dried
1 large clove garlic, crushed
26 ounces canned tomatoes
Pepper
⅔ cup dry white wine

Cut eggplant in half and score exposed sides. Sprinkle with salt and let stand for 30 minutes. Rinse and pat dry, then cut into chunks. Heat oil in a large skillet and fry onions until they are soft and just begin to brown. Stir in zucchini and red and green peppers; cook over low heat for 5 minutes. Remove from skillet and set aside. Put eggplant in skillet; cook 8 minutes or until eggplant just begins to brown. Add basil, garlic, tomatoes and pepper, bring to a boil and simmer 15 minutes until thickened. Add wine and cook 15 minutes more. Serve hot or cold.

To prepare peppers, halve them and remove the seeds and tough white membrane, then chop or slice them as required. Onions need to be peeled and halved, then sliced with a sharp knife. Wash zucchini, trim the ends and slice neatly into rings.

29

30

31

To remove tomato skins, cut a small cross in the skins and plunge them into boiling water for 10 seconds and then into cold water. The skins should peel away easily with a sharp knife.

Indian basmati rice has an excellent flavor and stays moist and separate. You can buy ground saffron or saffron strands. Crush saffron strands in a little boiling water before adding them to the dish.

Saffron Chicken

2 tablespoons olive oil
1 small chicken
Salt and pepper
1 onion, finely chopped
1 clove garlic, crushed
2 teaspoons paprika
8 tomatoes, peeled and
    chopped

1½ cups long-grain rice
4 cups boiling water
Large pinch of saffron
    strands or ½ teaspoon
    ground saffron
1 cup frozen peas
2 tablespoons chopped
    fresh parsley

Before starting recipe, cut chicken into 8 pieces. First, cut chicken in half lengthwise down the breastbone and through the backbone. Cut the halves in half again, slitting between the leg joint diagonally up and around the breast joint. Then cut away drumsticks from the leg thigh joint and wings from the breast joint to make 8 pieces. Remove skin by pulling and cutting with a sharp knife.

Heat oil in large flameproof casserole and fry chicken pieces for about 5 minutes or until brown. Season, remove from the casserole and set aside. Add onion and garlic to casserole and fry over low heat for 5 minutes until soft. Stir in paprika and fry for 30 seconds. Add tomatoes and cook for 10 minutes until slightly thickened. Stir in rice, water, saffron and chicken. Bring to a boil, then cover and simmer for about 15 minutes. Add peas and parsley and simmer for another 5 minutes until the rice is tender and the liquid has been absorbed.

April

*"When well-apparelled April on the heel
Of limping Winter treads."*

William Shakespeare

Spring is here at last!
Refreshed by April showers, the garden begins to
blossom and new vegetables appear almost daily. April
has a wonderful variety – the weather may be cold and
blustery or pleasantly warm and breezy. In the kitchen,
too, cooks offer warming fish dishes on colder days and
provide a tempting foretaste of summer with the earliest
beans and salad vegetables.

APRIL

1

The oldest April fool breakfast is the empty egg shell upside down in its cup and beautifully served with hot toast.

5

2

6

Toss lightly steamed broccoli in 2 tablespoons olive oil and 2 teaspoons anchovy paste until hot for an unusual side dish.

3

7

4

Make chili flowers from small green or red chilies to decorate oriental dishes. Slit the chilies lengthwise from the tip, leaving about 1 inch of the stalk end intact. Scrape out the seeds and fibrous portions. Stand the chilies in a bowl of ice water for 1 hour until they curl into flowers.

Spicy Noodles

12 Chinese dried
  mushrooms
8 ounces Chinese egg
  noodles
5 tablespoons oil
4 carrots, thinly sliced
2 cups broccoli florets
1 clove garlic

4 green onions, diagonally
  sliced
1 teaspoon chili
4 tablespoons soy sauce
4 tablespoons rice wine or
  dry sherry
2 teaspoons cornstarch

Soak mushrooms in warm water for about 30 minutes.
Meanwhile, cook noodles in boiling salted water for about 5
minutes. Drain, rinse under hot water and drain again. Toss
with 1 tablespoon of oil. Blanch carrots and broccoli in boiling
water for 2 minutes. Drain and rinse under cold water. Drain
mushrooms, discard stems and slice the caps. Heat remaining
oil with the garlic in a wok then remove the garlic. Add
carrots and broccoli and stir-fry for 1 minute. Add mushrooms
and green onions and stir-fry for 2 minutes. Mix together the
chili sauce, soy sauce, wine or sherry and cornstarch. Pour
over the vegetables and stir-fry until the sauce clears. Add
noodles and toss together until heated through.

You can use any type of
egg noodles for this dish,
or use rice noodles. Both
are available dried in
various thicknesses in
specialty food shops. In
China they are a symbol of
longevity and are often
served at birthday parties as
a wish for long life.

APRIL

8

For a tasty buffet dish, purée some light pâté and whipped cream until soft and fill little rolls of ham.

12

9

13

To make sweet eggs, color tiny pieces of marzipan with food coloring and roll in mixed spice for a speckled effect.

10

14

11

This recipe makes a perfect appetizer snack or canapé. It is delicious served cold, and makes an attractive dish for a picnic or buffet table. You do not have to stick to hen's eggs. Quail, duck, goose or bantam eggs work equally well.

Stuffed Eggs

4 eggs
1 cup cooked minced
  ham
4 tablespoons grated mild
  cheese
4 tablespoons cream
2 teaspoons prepared
  mustard

Salt and pepper
2 teaspoons chopped fresh
  dill or chives
3 tablespoons bread crumbs
2 tablespoons butter, melted
1 sprig fresh parsley

Pierce large end of each egg and lower into boiling water. As water returns to a boil, roll eggs around for 2 minutes to help set yolks; cook 8 minutes more. Drain, rinse and leave in cold water. Remove shells, cut eggs in half lengthwise and remove yolks. Mix yolks with all remaining ingredients except bread crumbs, butter and parsley. Spoon mixture back into egg whites. Sprinkle on bread crumbs and drizzle with melted butter. Place under broiler for 3 minutes or until crisp and golden brown. Garnish with parsley.

15

16

Brush a whole, cleaned bluefish with oil, season with dried oregano and bake in a 350° F oven for 25 minutes.

17

18

19

20

Scatter cubes of your favorite hard cheese over a layer of tomato slices and top with olive oil and pepper.

21

There are many different varieties of lettuce now available, from the familiar iceberg, romaine and leaf to the more unusual chicory escarole, French endive and lamb's lettuce. Try a selection to find your favorites. The darker-leaved varieties tend to be slightly bitter, so use them sparingly.

Spring Salad

1¾ cups cottage cheese
1 carrot, coarsely grated
8 radishes, coarsely grated
2 green onions, thinly
  sliced
Salt and pepper

1 teaspoon chopped fresh dill
  or marjoram
⅔ cup sour cream or
  thick yogurt
Selection of lettuce leaves
4 sprigs fresh dill

Strain excess liquid from cottage cheese while you prepare
the vegetables. Mix together all ingredients except the lettuce
leaves and dill sprigs. Chill for about 20 minutes. To serve,
arrange a selection of lettuce leaves and a mound of salad on
individual plates and garnish with sprigs of dill. Serve with
thinly sliced rye, whole-wheat or French bread and butter.

Grate the vegetables on the
coarse side of the grater to
create short strips that
will absorb the flavors of
the salad while retaining
their crispness.
If you are making
a larger quantity, it
may be quicker to
use a food
processor.

APRIL

22

23

24

Scoop the insides out of baked potatoes, mix with butter and egg, spoon back into the shells and bake until golden.

25

26

Fry diced cooked lamb in butter with chopped bacon, onion, parsley, fried potato and Worcestershire sauce; top with fried eggs.

27

28

Make another delicious lamb stuffing by frying 1 small chopped onion in a little butter then mixing it with the grated peel and juice of 1 orange, 4 tablespoons bread crumbs, ½ cup mixed golden raisins and currants and a little rosemary and thyme, salt and pepper.

Stuffed Lamb

Half breast of lamb
1 onion
Salt and pepper
1 cup bread crumbs
1 ounce ground suet
½ teaspoon dried marjoram

½ teaspoon dried thyme
Grated peel of ½ lemon
1 egg
1 tablespoon flour
2 sprigs fresh parsley

Heat oven to 400°F. Bone the lamb. Place bones in a saucepan with half the onion and some salt and pepper. Cover with water, bring to a boil, skim, cover and simmer for 30 minutes. Strain and reserve stock. Finely chop the remaining onion and mix with the bread crumbs, suet, herbs, lemon peel, salt, pepper, egg and 2 tablespoons of stock. Spread the stuffing over the lamb, roll up and tie firmly with string. Bake in a greased roasting pan for 1 hour. Transfer meat to a warm serving dish and keep it warm. Drain off any excess fat from the pan, stir in flour and cook for 1 minute. Stir in 1 cup of stock, bring to a boil, stirring constantly, and boil for 3 minutes. Strain into a gravy boat. Garnish lamb with parsley and serve with new potatoes and zucchini.

For a deliciously creamy and unusual sauce, use slightly less stock for the gravy and mix in 4 tablespoons red currant jelly and 4 tablespoons cream, seasoning to taste. Slice the lamb, arrange the slices on a warm platter and pour on the sauce before serving.

29

30

Salmon steaks make a great meal simply brushed with melted butter and crushed garlic and broiled until tender.

The best way to cook fresh salmon is to poach it in a court bouillon. Finely chop 2 carrots, 1 onion, 2 stalks celery and 2 shallots and mix with 1 bay leaf, 3 parsley stalks, 2 sprigs fresh thyme, 2 tablespoons lemon juice 1¼ cups dry white wine and 4 cups water. Cover and simmer for 15 minutes. Meanwhile, cut the fins and gills off the cleaned fish, cut an inverted V into the tail and wash it well. Strain the court bouillon over the fish in a buttered ovenproof dish or fish kettle. Cover and poach in a preheated 350°F oven, allowing about 8 minutes per pound, until fish flakes when tested with a fork.

Leave to cool in the court bouillon, then remove the fish. Cut the skin just below the head and above the tail and carefully peel off the skin. Cut the backbone below the head and above the tail, then split the fish along the backbone with a sharp knife. Ease the bone out from the back without breaking the fish. Salmon steaks can be poached in the same way.

You can add a little chopped dill to the flan if you wish. An attractive feathery herb, it is often used with fish dishes because of its delicate flavor. Dill seeds are also available but these have a stronger taste.

Salmon Flan

6 ounces frozen puff pastry	*Salt and pepper*
2 teaspoons cornstarch	*1 tablespoon butter*
⅔ cup milk	*(optional)*
6 ounces cooked fresh	*1 egg, beaten*
or canned salmon	*4 sprigs fresh dill*

Heat oven to 375°F. Roll out the pastry and line a greased 8-inch flan dish. Mix the cornstarch with a little milk. Bring the remaining milk to a boil, stir into the cornstarch mixture and return to the pan. Cook for 1 minute, stirring constantly. Season with salt and pepper. Mix butter into the fresh salmon or drain the canned salmon and flake the fish, removing any bones or skin. Remove sauce from heat, beat in the egg, then fold in the salmon and spoon mixture into the pastry shell. Bake for 40 minutes. Serve garnished with dill sprigs with a crisp salad and whole-wheat bread or baked potatoes and baby peas.

May

*"And the May month flaps its glad green leaves like wings,
Delicate-filmed as new-spun silk."*

Thomas Hardy

Spring is flourishing and summer buds are shooting up, while a special seasonal treat, asparagus, brings its delicate flavor into the kitchen. The first deliciously tender vegetables are available; fruits begin to soften and ripen, with strawberries, melons and other luscious offerings from California. Once May is here, summer is just around the corner and you can put away your winter coats.

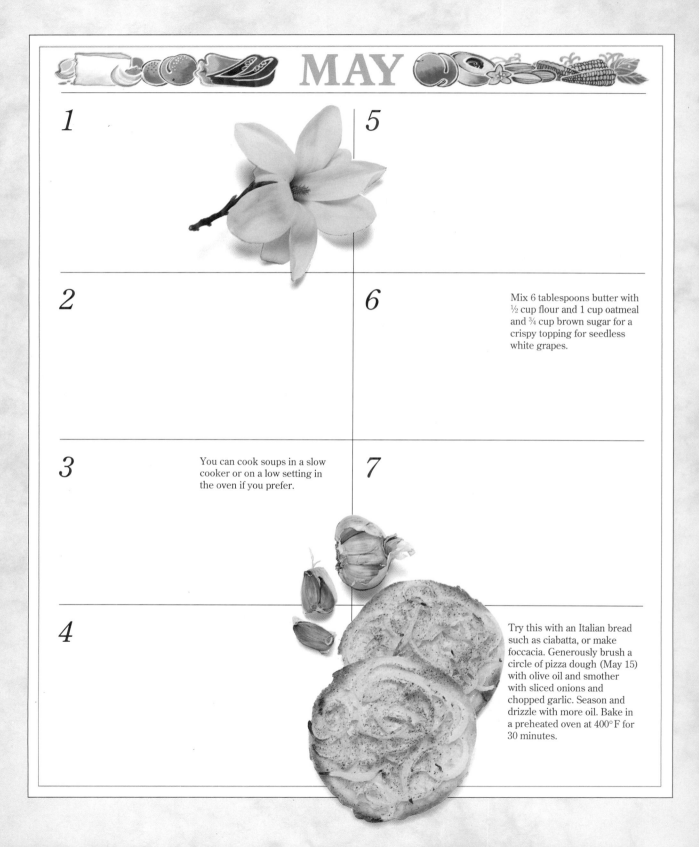

MAY

1

5

2

6

Mix 6 tablespoons butter with ½ cup flour and 1 cup oatmeal and ¾ cup brown sugar for a crispy topping for seedless white grapes.

3

You can cook soups in a slow cooker or on a low setting in the oven if you prefer.

7

4

Try this with an Italian bread such as ciabatta, or make foccacia. Generously brush a circle of pizza dough (May 15) with olive oil and smother with sliced onions and chopped garlic. Season and drizzle with more oil. Bake in a preheated oven at 400°F for 30 minutes.

Minestrone means "big soup." For a thinner soup, omit the pasta and reduce the amount of vegetables.

Minestrone

⅔ cup navy beans
5 cups vegetable stock
2 tablespoons olive oil
1 onion, finely chopped
1 clove garlic, crushed
1 stalk celery, thinly sliced
2 carrots, diced
⅔ cup green beans
1 cup salad greens, shredded
1 zucchini, diced

⅔ cup tomatoes, peeled and diced
1 bay leaf
1 cup pasta shells
Salt and pepper
1 tablespoon chopped fresh basil
1 tablespoon chopped fresh parsley

Soak beans overnight in the stock. Heat oil and fry the onion and garlic for 5 minutes until soft but not browned. Add vegetables and fry for 5 minutes until soft. Add beans and stock, tomatoes, bay leaf, pasta, salt and pepper. Bring to a boil, cover and simmer for 1 hour until beans are tender, stirring occasionally. Stir in the basil and parsley and heat through for 5 minutes. Serve with crusty bread.

There are many different recipes for minestrone, but they all make a substantial soup. You can substitute almost any vegetables of your choice, according to what is available. Any small shape of pasta is fine, or you can use broken pieces of spaghetti or long-grain rice.

MAY

8 Take advantage of the young carrots now available. Slice into strips and cook briefly so they are sweet and crisp.

12

9

13 To make herb oils for salads, place sprigs of basil, rosemary or bay in a bottle, fill with olive oil, seal and store for 4 weeks.

10

14 There is no limit to omelette ingredients! Try shrimp, corn, sliced mushrooms, grated cheese, chopped fresh herbs, diced potatoes, flaked salmon or salami. If the omelette is thick, do not fold it in half, but place it under a hot broiler until golden brown.

11

Ham and Pepper Omelette

3 eggs, beaten
2 tablespoons milk
Salt and pepper
3 tablespoons green pepper,
   chopped

2 tomatoes, peeled, seeded
   and chopped
½ cup ham, diced
1 tablespoon vegetable oil

Beat eggs, milk and salt and pepper. Heat the oil and fry the pepper for 5 minutes until soft. Stir in the tomatoes and ham and heat through for 1 minute. Pour in the egg mixture and stir well until it begins to cook. As the egg begins to set, lift it and tilt the pan to allow the uncooked egg to run underneath. When the underside is cooked and the top is still slightly creamy, fold the omelette in half and serve immediately with a crisp salad and crusty bread.

Green and red peppers, zucchini and any type of ham make excellent additions to omelettes. Chop them finely or coarsely, as you prefer, and fry them until they are just beginning to soften so they still have a slight crunch.

15

To obtain the right temperature of warm water when using yeast, use half boiling water and half tap water.

19

16

20

17

Broil pizza toppings on French bread for a quick snack or tasty dinner.

21

18

Other topping ingredients include Italian hams and sausages, tuna, clams, capers, zucchini, olives or Ricotta cheese. To make a calzone, brush the dough with olive oil and cover half with chopped ham and boiled egg, and cubes of Mozzarella. Fold in half, seal and brush with oil before baking.

Pizza Dough

1 teaspoon dry yeast
½ teaspoon sugar
¾ cup warm water
1⅓ cups flour
Pinch of salt
2 tablespoons olive
    oil

Mix the yeast and sugar in a small bowl, stir in the water and let stand for about 10 minutes until frothy. Sift the flour and salt into a bowl and make a well in the center. Add the oil and yeast mixture and mix the flour into the liquid to form a firm dough. Turn onto a floured surface and knead until smooth and elastic. Place in a lightly oiled bowl, cover and let stand in a warm place for 1 hour until doubled in size. Knead again and flatten the dough into a 10-inch circle.

Italian Pizza

2 tablespoons olive oil
1 onion, chopped
1 clove garlic, crushed
14 ounces canned tomatoes
1 tablespoon tomato paste
½ teaspoon dried oregano
½ teaspoon chopped fresh basil
1 teaspoon sugar
Salt and pepper

1 cup Mozzarella cheese,
    grated
¼ cup Parmesan cheese,
    grated
½ red pepper, sliced
½ green pepper, sliced
7 pitted black olives
2 ounces canned anchovies,
    drained

Heat oven to 400°F. Heat the oil in a skillet and fry the onion and garlic for 5 minutes until soft but not browned. Add the tomatoes and juice, tomato paste, herbs, sugar, salt and pepper. Bring to a boil and simmer until thick and smooth, stirring occasionally. Allow to cool. Spread the sauce over the dough, sprinkle half the cheese, then arrange the peppers, olives and anchovies on top. Sprinkle with the remaining cheese and bake for 20 minutes.

MAY

22

When cooking rice, fill a measuring cup with 1¼ cups rice for 4 people and use twice the amount of water.

26

23

27

24

Soak dried fruits in boiling water for about 10 minutes to plump them up; then drain well before use.

28

25

As an alternate dressing, whisk together 4 tablespoons dry sherry, 3 tablespoons olive oil, 2 tablespoons white wine vinegar, 1 teaspoon lemon juice and some salt and pepper. Season dressings with a sprinkling of chopped fresh herbs if you wish.

Rice and Nut Salad

2 tablespoons olive oil
2 tablespoons lemon juice
Salt and pepper
½ cup golden raisins, plumped
¼ cup currants, plumped
1¼ cups cooked brown rice
3 ounces almonds, chopped

2 ounces walnuts, chopped
2 ounces cashew nuts, chopped
15 ounces peach slices in natural juice, drained and chopped
¼ cucumber, cubed
½ cup cooked red kidney beans
6 pitted black olives

You can substitute apricot or kiwi fruit for the peaches if you prefer, and of course you can use fresh fruit if it is available. Whatever you choose, this makes a highly nutritious salad that is perfect for a lunch or dinner dish.

Put the olive oil, lemon juice, salt and pepper in a screw-top jar and shake vigorously until thickened. Mix together the plumped fruits, rice, nuts, peaches, cucumber, beans and olives. Pour on the dressing and toss thoroughly. Serve on a bed of shredded crisp lettuce or endive.

29

31

30

Feta cheese is a soft, white, Greek cheese made with ewes' or goats' milk. You can substitute a creamy cheese such as Ricotta or even a crumbled mild English cheese such as Caerphilly for this recipe if you prefer.

To prepare spinach, tear off the stalks by holding the leaves firmly and pulling the stems backwards. Wash the leaves thoroughly, drain well, then shred them with a sharp knife. If you use frozen spinach, simply heat through the thawed spinach with the softened onions then leave to cool.

You can make a delicious Spinach and Onion Quiche using the same onion and spinach mixture. Line a quiche pan with shortcrust pastry and spread in the onion mixture. Beat 3 eggs with 4 tablespoons light cream and 4 tablespoons milk and pour over the flan. Season with freshly grated nutmeg and bake in a preheated oven at 400° F for 30 minutes.

Spinach and Feta Pie

½ pound phyllo dough
1 pound spinach
2 tablespoons olive oil
1 onion, finely chopped
1 tablespoon chopped fresh dill

3 eggs, beaten
4 ounces feta cheese
Salt and pepper
4 tablespoons butter, melted

Heat oven to 375° F. Cut phyllo leaves to fit your baking pan and cover with a damp cloth. Prepare the spinach. Heat oil in skillet and fry onion for 5 minutes until soft. Add spinach and stir for 5 minutes over medium heat; increase heat to evaporate moisture. Allow to cool, then mix in dill, eggs, cheese, salt and pepper. Brush melted butter in baking pan. Brush 8 phyllo leaves with butter; lay in bottom of dish. Spread on filling and cover with remaining leaves, brushing each one with melted butter and scoring the top into diamond shapes. Sprinkle with water and bake for 40 minutes until crisp and golden. Leave to stand 10 minutes. Cut into wedges and serve with crisp lettuce leaves.

Phyllo dough is available in frozen packages already rolled into thin sheets. It is easy to handle, but must be covered with a damp cloth to keep it moist while you are preparing the dish. Brush lightly with sunflower oil rather than butter if you prefer.

June

"A noise like of a hidden brook,
In the leafy month of June,
That to the sleeping woods all night
Singeth a quiet tune."
Samuel Taylor Coleridge

J UNE – such a relaxing time of year. The weather warms, days are long and the fresh scents of early summer are everywhere. The color green has more shades than you ever imagined. You can hardly decide which salad vegetables to buy, since they all look so delicious. Each time you turn around something new appears in the garden and in the kitchen. It's the perfect month to bring variety to the table.

JUNE

1

5

Mix 4 ounces chopped shrimp, 4 tablespoons butter, ½ teaspoon curry powder and 1 tablespoon chopped parsley, spread on toast and broil lightly.

2

Peanut oil is perfect for stir-frying since it has a mild taste and can be heated to high temperatures.

6

3

7

4

Chinese rice wine is made from glutinous rice, yeast and spring water. It is widely used in China for cooking and drinking. You can buy it in specialty food shops – be sure it is tightly corked and stored at room temperature. You can substitute a dry sherry.

Quick-Fried Shrimp

2 pounds cooked shrimp
1 tablespoon finely chopped
  ginger root
1 tablespoon chopped fresh
  coriander
3 tablespoons peanut oil
1 tablespoon rice wine or
  dry sherry
2 tablespoons light soy sauce
2 cloves garlic, crushed
4 green onions, sliced

Shell the shrimp, leaving on the tails. Place in a bowl with all
the remaining ingredients except green onions. Allow to
marinate for 30 minutes. Heat a wok and add shrimp and
marinade. Stir-fry for a few minutes until heated through.
Sprinkle with green onions and serve.

You can also make
this recipe using equal
amount of shrimp
and scallops.

8

9

10

Mix Ricotta cheese with chopped fresh basil and use it to fill bottled cherry peppers. Serve as a cocktail snack.

11

12

13

Dress up a bowl of soft vanilla ice cream with a topping of puréed fruit and chopped nuts.

14

Make Pepper and Pasta Salad by frying 2 sliced peppers with 1 sliced onion, 2 sliced zucchini, a clove of garlic and 2 peeled tomatoes. Mix with cooked pasta spirals, season and top with oil and vinegar. Serve the salad with prosciutto ham or salami, crusty bread and dry white wine.

Pepper Sunburst

2 red peppers
2 green peppers
2 yellow peppers
6 tablespoons vegetable oil
1 tablespoon white wine
  vinegar
1 small clove garlic, crushed

Pinch of salt
Pinch of cayenne pepper
Pinch of sugar
2 hard-boiled eggs
18 pitted black olives
1 tablespoon chopped fresh
  coriander

You can use any color pepper for this salad, and roast them in a hot oven instead of under the broiler. To shorten preparation time, use bottled or canned peppers, drain them thoroughly and slice them into strips.

Cut peppers in half and remove seeds; press down to flatten. Brush skin side with a little oil and broil until skin begins to char and split. Place peppers in a loosely-tied plastic bag and leave for 15 minutes. Whisk together remaining oil, wine vinegar, garlic, salt, cayenne pepper and sugar. Cut eggs into wedges. Remove pepper from the bag, peel away the skin and cut pepper into thick strips. Arrange on a serving plate with eggs and olives. Sprinkle with coriander and spoon on the dressing. Chill for 1 hour before serving.

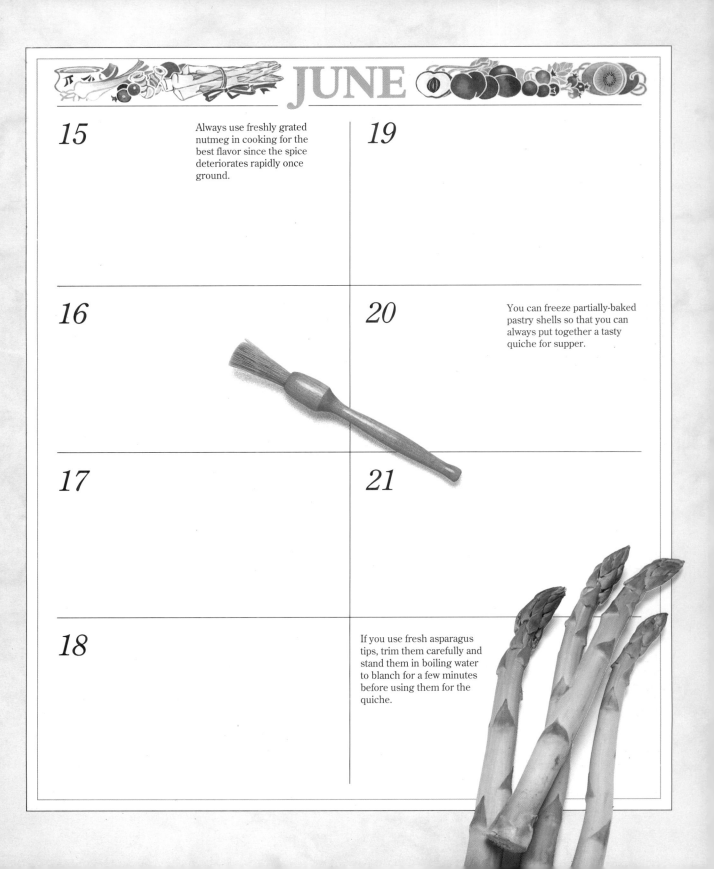

JUNE

15

Always use freshly grated nutmeg in cooking for the best flavor since the spice deteriorates rapidly once ground.

19

16

20

You can freeze partially-baked pastry shells so that you can always put together a tasty quiche for supper.

17

21

18

If you use fresh asparagus tips, trim them carefully and stand them in boiling water to blanch for a few minutes before using them for the quiche.

Asparagus Quiche

4 tablespoons shortening
6 tablespoons butter
1⅓ cups flour
3 tablespoons water
3 eggs
1¼ cups light cream
Pinch of freshly ground
   nutmeg
Salt and pepper
2 tablespoons flour

8 ounces canned
   asparagus tips
½ cup pitted green olives
1 onion, chopped and fried
   in butter
⅔ cup Cheddar cheese,
   grated
1 tablespoon Parmesan
   cheese, grated

Any hard cheese is suitable for this quiche. Try to buy fresh Parmesan and grate it yourself for the best flavor. Grated Parmesan in containers doesn't taste the same.

Heat oven to 375° F. Cut shortening and 4 tablespoons of butter into flour; add enough water to make a pastry. Roll out and line a 10-inch quiche dish. Cover with parchment paper; fill with baking beans and bake for 10 minutes. Remove beans and paper. Whisk together eggs, cream, nutmeg, salt and pepper in a bowl. Blend a small portion of this mixture with flour and return to the bowl; stir. Arrange asparagus, olives and onion in pastry shell, pour on cream and sprinkle with cheese. Dot with remaining butter and bake for 25 minutes. Reduce heat to 350° F and bake for 15 minutes more or until quiche is golden brown.

22

23

Add 3 tablespoons of rum to puréed mango to give extra flavor for special occasions.

24

25

26

27

Blend together 4 tablespoons gin, 4 tablespoons coconut cream, 4 strawberries and 2 scoops crushed ice for an exotic summer cocktail.

28

When you are preparing fruit for a salad, always slice or cut it to show its most attractive side. Slice kiwi fruit crosswise to reveal its stunning color and pattern. Slice starfruit thinly and maintain its pretty shape. Cut passion fruit in half with a zig-zag pattern.

Exotic Fruit Salad

3 ripe peaches
3 kiwi fruits
1 starfruit
¾ cup ripe strawberries

2 ripe mangoes
Juice of ½ lime
⅔ cup red currants
Strawberry leaves

Plunge peaches into boiling water for a few seconds and carefully peel away skin using a sharp knife. Remove pits and cut into slices. Peel and slice kiwi fruits. Trim and slice starfruit. Leave stems on strawberries and cut in half lengthwise. Arrange fruit on a serving platter. Peel mangoes, remove pits, chop and purée with lime juice and half of the redcurrants. Strain purée through a sieve. Sprinkle remaining red currants over the fruit, pour the puréed mango over it and garnish with strawberry leaves. Chill for at least 1 hour before serving.

Raspberries, apricots, cherries, plums, blackberries, grapes, pineapple, passion fruit and guava are all ideal for this wonderful salad.

29

30

Top cooked diced beets with ½ cup sherry, 1 teaspoon sugar, 1 tablespoon wine vinegar, salt and pepper and chill for 30 minutes.

Another wonderful Mexican dish is Chili con Carne. Soften 2 chopped onions in 3 tablespoons oil. Add 1 crushed clove garlic, 2 teaspoons each ground cumin and paprika and 1 chopped green chili. Cook for 1 minute. Add 1 pound lean ground beef, allow to brown, and stir in 14 ounces canned tomatoes, 3 tablespoons tomato paste, 1 teaspoon dried oregano, 1 bay leaf and ½ cup beer. Cover and simmer for 1 hour, stirring occasionally. Stir in ½ cup each canned red kidney beans, pinto beans and Garbanzo beans and cook for 15 minutes more.

Mexican Seviche

1 pound cod fillets
Juice and grated peel of
  2 limes
1 shallot, chopped
1 green chili pepper, seeded
  and chopped
1 teaspoon ground coriander
1 green pepper, sliced
1 red pepper, sliced
1 tablespoon chopped fresh parsley
1 tablespoon chopped fresh
  coriander
4 green onions, chopped
2 tablespoons olive oil
Salt and pepper
1 head lettuce, shredded

Skin cod and cut into thin strips across the grain. Place in a bowl and pour on lime juice. Add peel, shallot, chili pepper and coriander; stir well. Cover and chill for 24 hours, stirring occasionally. To serve, drain fish and stir in the green and red peppers, herbs, onions and oil. Season to taste and serve on a bed of lettuce.

Don't be deterred by the thought of eating raw fish, because the cod will "cook" in the spicy marinade and the result is absolutely delicious.

Serve the salad with a bowl of crispy tortilla chips, which give a wonderful contrast in flavor and texture.

July

"Summertime, and the livin' is easy,
Fish are jumpin', an' the cotton is high."

Dubose Heyward

T HE pleasures of summer
are outdoor ones – baseball games, bicycling, hiking and
long days at the seashore all create hearty appetites.
Food moves outside as well, to the backyard barbecue.
What would July Fourth be without an outdoor feast
under blue skies and billowing clouds? Save the warmth
of the kitchen for showery and overcast days, when you
can make pies and preserves from the strawberries and
raspberries you picked on brighter days.

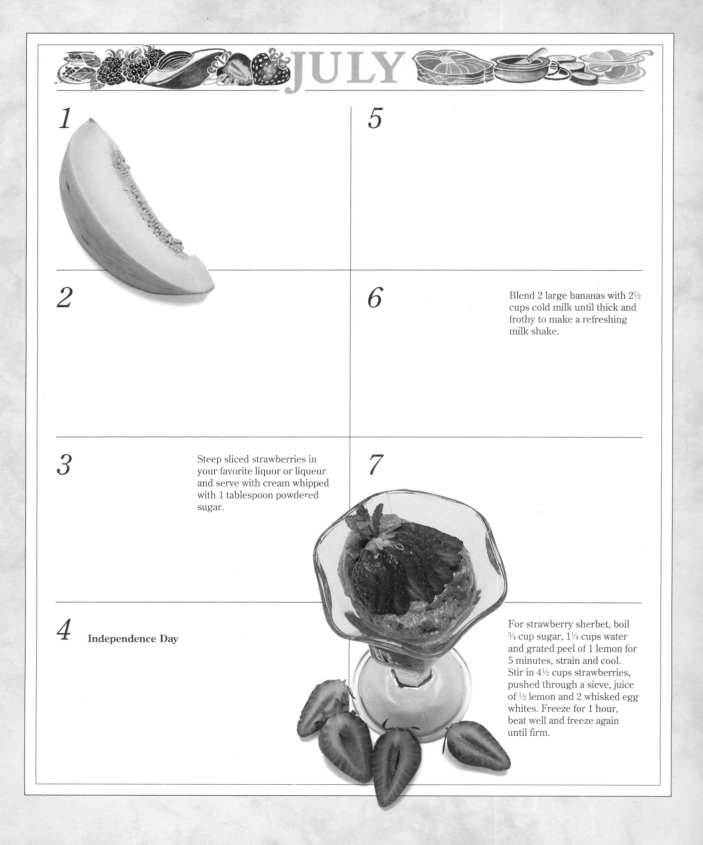

JULY

1

2

3

Steep sliced strawberries in your favorite liquor or liqueur and serve with cream whipped with 1 tablespoon powdered sugar.

4 Independence Day

5

6

Blend 2 large bananas with 2½ cups cold milk until thick and frothy to make a refreshing milk shake.

7

For strawberry sherbet, boil ¾ cup sugar, 1¼ cups water and grated peel of 1 lemon for 5 minutes, strain and cool. Stir in 4½ cups strawberries, pushed through a sieve, juice of ½ lemon and 2 whisked egg whites. Freeze for 1 hour, beat well and freeze again until firm.

Strawberry Frost

*3 cups strawberries,
    hulled*
1 large banana
¾ cup plain yogurt

*A few drops of vanilla
    extract*
1 teaspoon honey

Put half the strawberries in the refrigerator.
Halve or quarter the remaining strawberries,
cut banana into chunks and freeze
them together until solid. Just
before serving, place the frozen
strawberries and bananas in a
blender or food processor with
the yogurt, vanilla extract and
honey. Process until smooth,
pushing the mixture down
2 or 3 times. Divide between
individual serving dishes
and garnish with the
reserved strawberries.
Serve at once.

Strawberries are at their
best in early summer, when
they are ripe, red and juicy
with plenty of flavor. For a
change, the recipe also
tastes delicious made with
raspberries.

8

Throw a few herb sprigs on the barbecue coals when you are broiling to give simple foods added flavor.

12

9

13

Bite-size rounds of lamb are perfect for the barbecue. They can be marinated in oil and herbs or just sprinkled with herbs, brushed with oil and broiled.

10

14

11

To make Spiced Tomato Juice, mix 3 cups tomato juice, ⅔ cup water, 1 tablespoon each sugar and lemon juice, 1 teaspoon each Worcestershire sauce and ground cloves, ½ teaspoon cayenne pepper and a pinch of salt. Simmer for 20 minutes. Strain and chill.

Lamb Kebabs

½ pound lean lamb
Juice of 1 lemon
3 tablespoons olive oil
1 clove garlic, crushed
½ tablespoon dried oregano

½ tablespoon dried thyme
Salt and pepper
12 bay leaves
2 onions, sliced into rings

Cut lamb into 2-inch cubes and place in a bowl. Mix together the lemon juice, oil, garlic, herbs, salt and pepper. Pour over meat and stir well. Cover and marinate in a cool place for at least 4 hours. Thread the lamb onto skewers alternately with bay leaves. Slip onion rings over meat. Broil for about 10 minutes; turn frequently and baste with marinade. Serve with rice and salad.

You can add other vegetables to the kebabs if you wish. Chunks of pepper, mushrooms, onion wedges and zucchini slices are delicious with lamb. To prevent wooden skewers from charring while cooking, soak them in water before preparing the kebabs.

Make kebabs with kidneys, fish, chicken, turkey, pork or beef. Choose ingredients that take about the same time to cook.

15

19

For the best flavor, buy corn-fed chicken.

16

Make a summer cocktail with Campari poured over crushed ice in a tall glass topped with fresh orange juice.

20

17

21

18

To remove an avocado pit, cut the avocado lengthwise, twist the two halves apart and lift the pit out. To prevent the avocado from turning brown, always prepare it at the last minute and coat with lemon juice.

Chicken and Avocado Salad

8 anchovy fillets
6 tablespoons milk
1 green onion, chopped
2 tablespoons chopped fresh
  tarragon or 1 tablespoon
  dried
3 tablespoons snipped fresh
  chives
4 tablespoons chopped fresh
  parsley

1¼ cups mayonnaise
2 tablespoons tarragon
  vinegar
⅔ cup plain yogurt
Pinch of sugar
Pinch of cayenne pepper
1 head lettuce, shredded
3 cups diced cooked chicken
1 avocado
1 tablespoon lemon juice

Soak anchovy fillets in milk for 30 minutes. Drain, rinse and pat dry. Set aside lettuce, chicken, avocado and lemon juice. Purée all the remaining ingredients in a blender or food processor and refrigerate for at least 1 hour. Arrange lettuce in a serving bowl, add chicken and spoon the dressing on. Remove skin and pit from the avocado, cut in cubes and immediately toss in lemon juice. Sprinkle avocado over salad and serve.

This dressing can be served with a tossed green salad or as a dip for raw vegetables.

Cut fresh carrots, cucumber and peppers into julienne strips and cauliflower into tiny florets and arrange attractively around a small bowl of dip.

JULY

22

23

Fold puréed summertime fruits into whipped cream and serve with crunchy cookies for a simple summer dessert.

24

25

26

Sliced tomatoes are delicious layered with a sprinkling of sugar. Pour vinaigrette dressing over them and chill for 1 hour.

27

28

A more unusual Spanish cold soup can be made by pounding 3 ounces almonds and 1 clove garlic to a fine paste with a little water. Beat in 1 cup fresh bread crumbs, 6 tablespoons olive oil, 1 tablespoon wine vinegar and 2½ cups water. Season to taste and serve chilled.

As a garnish for the soup, chop 1 onion, ½ cucumber, 3 peeled tomatoes and ½ green pepper. Arrange some of the garnish on top of the soup and offer the rest separately. You can also use croutons, chopped green onions, red onions or red peppers.

Originally, gazpacho was pounded in a mortar and pestle in huge quantities to feed hungry farm workers returning from the fields.

Gazpacho

1 green pepper, chopped
8 tomatoes, peeled, seeded
  and chopped
1 large cucumber, peeled
  and chopped
1 large onion, chopped
½ loaf French bread,
  crusts removed

3 cups water
Salt and pepper
2 cloves garlic, crushed
3 tablespoons olive oil
2 tablespoons tomato
  paste (optional)
3 tablespoons red wine
  vinegar

Break bread into small pieces and place in a bowl. Add vegetables and mix together. Add wine vinegar, water, salt, pepper and garlic. Purée mixture until smooth; blend batches separately if necessary. Beat in oil and tomato paste, if desired. Cover and chill for at least 2 hours. Mix thoroughly with a whisk before serving.

29

30

Try an Indian Carrot and Grape Salad. Cut 3 carrots into julienne strips and mix with 1½ cups seedless grapes. Mix 2 tablespoons oil, 1 tablespoon honey, 1 tablespoon white wine vinegar, 2 teaspoons lemon juice, 1 teaspoon crushed mustard seeds and a pinch of pepper. Toss with the carrots and grapes and sprinkle with paprika.

31

Curries do not have to be very hot. A mild chicken curry made with banana, pineapple or coconut makes a good summer meal.

Chilled Fish Curry

8 ounces salmon fillets
12 ounces white fish
  fillets
1¼ cups fish or chicken
  stock
Salt and pepper
½ cup mayonnaise
2 cups plain yogurt

2 teaspoons curry powder
Juice and grated peel of
  ½ lemon
4 ounces cooked peeled
  shrimp
1 kiwi fruit, sliced
1 sprig fresh mint
1 tablespoon flaked coconut

Place fish in a shallow skillet and cover with stock. Season to taste with salt and pepper. Simmer for 15 minutes until fish is just cooked. Remove fish from liquid and allow to cool slightly. Mix together mayonnaise, yogurt, curry powder, lemon juice and peel. Separate fish into flakes and remove bones. Mix fish into the sauce and add shrimp. Garnish with kiwi fruit, mint and coconut flakes. Serve with boiled rice or new potatoes and a mixed salad.

There are many types of rice available. Brown rice is the unprocessed grain and needs more water and a longer cooking time.

Long-grain rice cooks into separate fluffy grains and is an excellent accompaniment to meat and fish. Wild rice is especially good with game and poultry.

August

*"The paired butterflies are already yellow with August
Over the grass in the West garden."*

Ezra Pound

O RCHARD and field offer a
plentitude of luscious choice. The weather remains
alluring, and the barbecues continue. With such a variety
of food on hand, this is the perfect time to expand the
cooking repertoire. This month's recipes offer some
unusual opportunities to be creative. Slow, hot days will
give you the time to dabble in dishes with international
flavors and enliven your table.

AUGUST

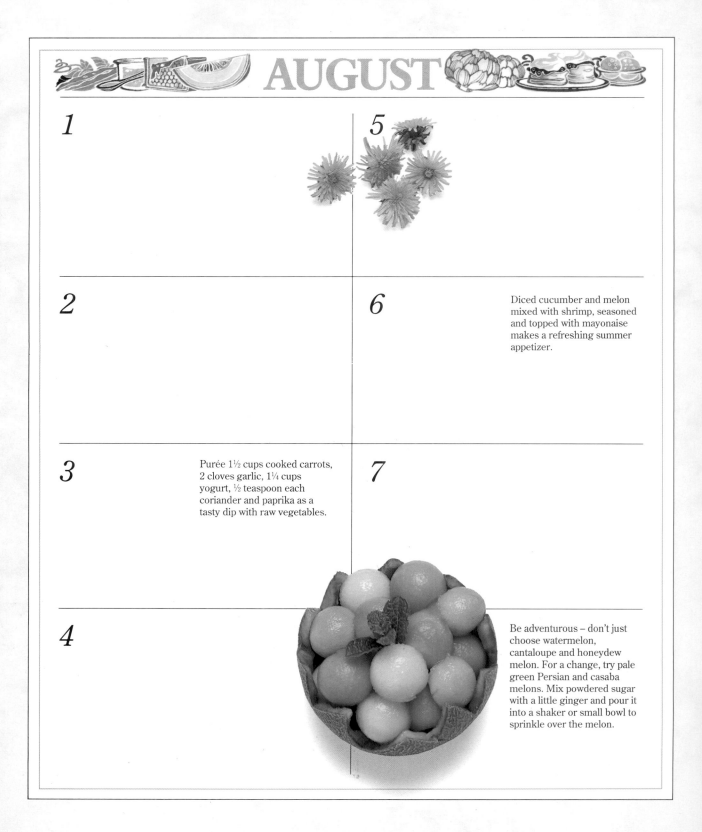

1

2

3

Purée 1½ cups cooked carrots, 2 cloves garlic, 1¼ cups yogurt, ½ teaspoon each coriander and paprika as a tasty dip with raw vegetables.

4

5

6

Diced cucumber and melon mixed with shrimp, seasoned and topped with mayonaise makes a refreshing summer appetizer.

7

Be adventurous – don't just choose watermelon, cantaloupe and honeydew melon. For a change, try pale green Persian and casaba melons. Mix powdered sugar with a little ginger and pour it into a shaker or small bowl to sprinkle over the melon.

Melon and Prosciutto

*1 large ripe honeydew
    melon*
16 thin slices prosciutto ham

*4 sprigs fresh flat-leafed
    parsley*

Cut melon in half, scoop out and discard seeds and fibers.
Peel away skin and cut the melon into 16 thin slices. Wrap
each piece in a slice of prosciutto and arrange on a serving
dish. Chill well and garnish with parsley before serving.

You can serve olives, stuffed
eggs and sliced salami with
this recipe if you wish, or
replace the melon with
fresh figs.

What we more often call
Parma ham is really
prosciutto crudo, for not all
prosciutto, in fact, comes
from Parma. The hams
are rubbed with a
mixture of salt, spices,
sugar and mustard
and matured to
produce a fine
quality raw ham.

AUGUST

8

9

Serve green beans cooked in boiling salted water until just tender and tossed with chopped onions fried in olive oil.

10

11

12 Buy tuna marked "dolphin friendly" to help stop fishermen from killing dolphins and other sea creatures caught in their drift nets.

13

14

For an unusual summer drink, purée 3 peeled mangoes with ½ teaspoon ground ginger, ½ teaspoon ground cinnamon, 1¼ cups orange juice and a dash of lemon juice. Serve in wine glasses decorated with thin slices of orange.

Salad Niçoise

1 head lettuce
1 hard-boiled egg, quartered
1 tomato, quartered
6 anchovy fillets
10 pitted black olives
1 tablespoon capers
¼ cucumber, diced
1 can tuna fish, drained

4 large artichoke hearts, quartered
6 tablespoons olive oil
2 tablespoons red wine vinegar
½ clove garlic, crushed
1 teaspoon mustard
1 teaspoon lemon juice

Wash lettuce thoroughly and tear into bite-sized pieces. Toss with other salad ingredients, taking care not to break up eggs. Whisk together dressing ingredients, add salt and pepper to taste and pour over the salad just before serving.

You can use frozen or canned artichoke hearts, but small tender fresh ones will need to be prepared. Cut off the stem, pull the leaves apart and scoop out the hairy choke. Remove the outer leaves down to the tender heart and drop into water with 1 tablespoon lemon juice.

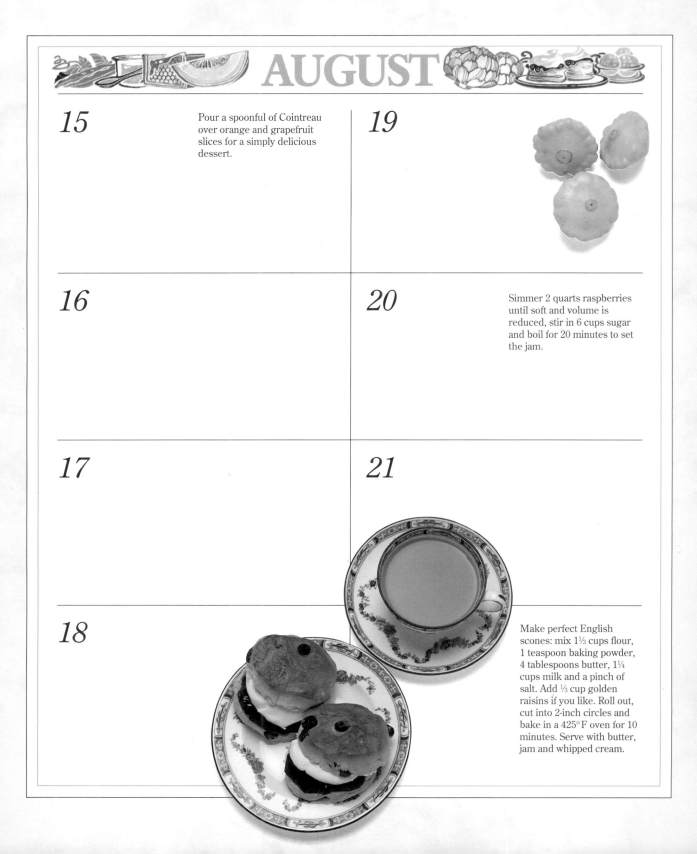

AUGUST

15

Pour a spoonful of Cointreau over orange and grapefruit slices for a simply delicious dessert.

19

16

20

Simmer 2 quarts raspberries until soft and volume is reduced, stir in 6 cups sugar and boil for 20 minutes to set the jam.

17

21

18

Make perfect English scones: mix 1⅓ cups flour, 1 teaspoon baking powder, 4 tablespoons butter, 1¼ cups milk and a pinch of salt. Add ⅓ cup golden raisins if you like. Roll out, cut into 2-inch circles and bake in a 425°F oven for 10 minutes. Serve with butter, jam and whipped cream.

Honey-Spice Oranges

1¼ cups honey
2 cups water
6 sprigs fresh mint

12 whole cloves
4 large oranges

Bring honey, water, 2 sprigs of mint and cloves to a boil in a heavy saucepan. Stir until honey has dissolved, then boil for 5 minutes until syrupy. Leave to cool, then strain. Pare the peel very thinly from 1 orange and cut into very fine shreds. Put the shreds into a bowl, cover with boiling water and let stand until cold. Drain well and stir into the syrup. Remove all skin and white membrane from oranges and slice into thin circles. Arrange on individual plates, pour on the chilled syrup and garnish with the remaining mint.

Honey gives sweetness as well as a delicious flavor to the syrup; try using a particular flower variety for a special taste. The syrup absorbs the flavor of the cloves and mint while boiling. Be sure to remove all fibrous material from orange, since it leaves a bitter aftertaste.

22

23

24

Dissolve 3 tablespoons sugar in 5 tablespoons water, pour over 4 peeled, cored and halved pears in a bowl and steam for 20 minutes.

25

26

27

Boil 8 ounces walnuts for 10 minutes, drain, dry, roll in ½ cup sugar and dry on a very low heat in the oven for 2 hours. Deep-fry until golden and allow to cool.

28

Chinese dried mushrooms add a distinctive flavor and aroma to Chinese dishes, and they can be used in this recipe instead of the pork. Soak mushrooms in hot water for about 30 minutes until soft; squeeze out excess moisture and remove the tough stems before slicing the caps.

Pork and Shrimp Chow Mein

8 ounces Chinese noodles
2 tablespoons peanut oil
8 ounces pork, sliced
1 carrot, shredded
1 red pepper, thinly sliced
¾ cup bean sprouts

½ cup snowpeas
1 tablespoon dry sherry
2 tablespoons soy sauce
4 ounces cooked peeled
shrimp

Cook the noodles in boiling salted water for about 5 minutes, rinse under hot water and drain well. Heat oil in a wok and stir-fry the pork for 5 minutes until almost cooked. Add the carrots and cook for 1 minute. Add pepper, bean sprouts, snowpeas, sherry and soy sauce and cook for 2 minutes. Add noodles and shrimp and toss over the heat for 2 minutes. Serve immediately.

Stir-fry blanched broccoli florets in 1 tablespoon oil with a small piece of grated ginger root to serve with this dish.

To make your own bean sprouts, wash 4 tablespoons mung beans, cover with cold water and soak overnight. Rinse in cold water, put into a clean glass jar and secure top with cheesecloth. Store in a warm dark dry place, rinsing the beans through the cheesecloth three times a day for about 4 days.

29

31

Insert a wooden pick into a chunk of cucumber. Start to slice it to the center, turning as you cut, to make a cucumber spiral garnish.

30

For a Sherry Cobbler, put plenty of crushed ice into a tall glass and half fill with sherry. Add a splash of orange Curaçao and a

teaspoon of fruit syrup and stir. Garnish with a sprig of fresh mint and a slice of orange and lemon.

To make a Summertime Soda, mix together the juice of 1 orange, 1 lemon and 1 grapefruit. Pour over ice cubes, add club soda and float a scoop of vanilla ice cream on top. Serve with straws and a spoon.

Coconut Cooler is another refreshing non-alcoholic drink. Mix 5 cups grapefruit juice, 5 cups pineapple juice and 1⅓ cups coconut milk. Chill well before serving.

Tipsy Cake

14 ounces canned fruit
   cocktail
5 tablespoons sweet sherry
8 almond cookies
12 ladyfingers
3 tablespoons raspberry jam
2 ounces sliced almonds

2 tablespoons cornstarch
2½ tablespoons sugar
2 drops vanilla extract
1¼ cups milk
1 egg, beaten
1¼ cups whipped cream
3 candied cherries, cut in half

Drain fruit. Mix a quarter of the juice with 4 tablespoons sherry. Set aside 4 cookies for decoration; crumble remainder. Spread jam on ladyfingers; arrange 4 in bottom of glass bowl. Cover with half the fruit, sprinkle with half the crumbled cookies and almonds; pour on one-third of juice and sherry mixture. Repeat, then top with remaining ladyfingers and juice.

Mix cornstarch and sugar with a little milk. Bring the rest of the milk almost to a boil, stir it into the cornstarch stirring constantly and simmer for 1 minute. Stir in remaining sherry and egg; cool until lukewarm. Pour over the cake, allowing some to trickle into the bowl. Chill well. Decorate with whipped cream, candied cherries and remaining cookies.

This is also a good way of using up angel food cake and white cake. Sliced gingerbread arranged in layers with sliced pears, seasoned with nutmeg and topped with custard also makes a delicious dessert.

September

*"The rule is, jam to-morrow and jam yesterday –
but never jam today."*

Lewis Carroll

Labor Day, and the last
chance for family outings before school begins.
September is the month for plums and apples, for
enjoying late summer nights. Use the longer evenings to
cook jams and chutneys for chilly winter days. Plan a
farewell-to-summer picnic – and get started on recipes for
the approaching fall and winter holidays. Fall is the time
to begin again, after a relaxing summer vacation. Try
more unusual dishes, especially those that incorporate
culinary traditions from all over the world.

SEPTEMBER

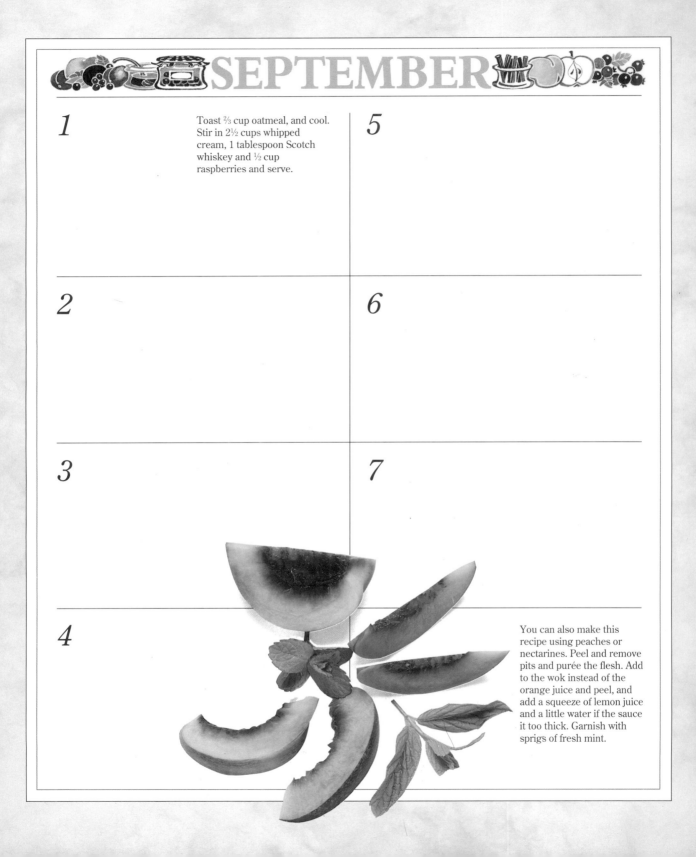

1

Toast ⅔ cup oatmeal, and cool. Stir in 2½ cups whipped cream, 1 tablespoon Scotch whiskey and ½ cup raspberries and serve.

5

2

6

3

7

4

You can also make this recipe using peaches or nectarines. Peel and remove pits and purée the flesh. Add to the wok instead of the orange juice and peel, and add a squeeze of lemon juice and a little water if the sauce it too thick. Garnish with sprigs of fresh mint.

Duck with Orange

3 oranges
1 duck
1 tablespoon butter
1 tablespoon vegetable oil
1¼ cups chicken stock
6 tablespoons dry red
 wine
2 tablespoons red currant
 jelly
Salt and pepper
1 teaspoon arrowroot
1 tablespoon water
1 sprig watercress

Remove peel from 2 of the oranges and cut into fine strips. Put peel in a bowl, cover with boiling water, allow to cool, then drain. Squeeze juice from 2 oranges. Peel and remove white inner pulp from the third orange and slice into thin circles.

Wash and dry the duck. Heat butter and oil in a wok and brown the duck all over. Remove duck from the wok, cool slightly and cut away the leg and wing ends. Cut duck in half lengthwise then cut each half into 1-inch strips. Remove fat from wok and return duck to the wok. Add stock, wine, red currant jelly, strips of orange peel and orange juice; bring to a boil and season to taste. Cover and simmer gently for 20 minutes or until well cooked. Skim any fat from surface. Mix arrowroot and water and stir it into the sauce. Bring back to a boil and simmer for 5 minutes until sauce is thick. Arrange on a warm serving plate and garnish with orange slices and watercress. Serve with roasted Duchess potatoes and green beans.

Use a sharp knife or poultry shears to cut the duck into 1-inch strips.

SEPTEMBER

8

9

Boil ½ cup sugar and ⅔ cup water and simmer grapefruit slices for 6 minutes. Add 4 tablespoons brandy and serve hot or cold.

10

11

12

Deep-fried herring makes an excellent appetizer. Fry in batches and serve hot with brown bread and butter.

13

14

Serve squid rings with a selection of dips. Make your own mayonnaise or use a name brand. Add to small bowls of mayonnaise: 1 clove garlic, crushed; 1 teaspoon curry powder; chopped mixed herbs; ½ chopped onion; 1 teaspoon Worcestershire sauce and ½ cup crumbled blue cheese.

Crispy Squid Rings

Lemon offers a sharp taste contrast to fried foods, especially with fresh parsley or oregano. A mixture of shrimp, shelled scallops and squid rings taste good cooked in this way. Do not overcook them or they will become rubbery.

1½ pound squid, cleaned and cut into rings
⅓ cup flour
Salt and pepper

Oil for deep-frying
1 lemon, cut into wedges
2 sprigs fresh parsley

Mix flour, salt and pepper and toss the squid in this mixture. Heat oil and fry squid in batches for about 3 minutes until golden brown and crisp. Drain on paper towels and sprinkle with salt. Arrange on a warm serving dish and garnish with lemon wedges and parsley.

SEPTEMBER

15

16

17

Core a tart cooking apple, slit around the skin, stuff with mincemeat and drizzle with honey. Bake in a moderate oven for 1 hour.

18

19

20

Serve plain yogurt with desserts as a delicious low-fat alternative to cream.

21

Make apple purée with cooking apples or any dessert apple. Wash, peel and core 1 pound apples; cut into quarters. Place in saucepan, adding 3 tablespoons water and some grated lemon peel. Simmer until apples are soft. Strain through a sieve or purée in a food processor.

Apple and Honey Tart

6 tablespoons butter
½ cup whole-wheat flour
½ cup white flour
3 egg yolks
3 tablespoons water

1¼ cups apple purée
4 tablespoons honey
2 tablespoons ground almonds
2 eating apples, thinly sliced

Heat oven to 375° F and grease a 9-inch pie plate or tart pan. Cream butter and flour together in a bowl. Beat 1 egg yolk with 2 tablespoons water and add to the mixture to form a soft dough; add more water if needed. Roll out dough and line pan; prick bottom crust with fork and flute edges. Mix apple purée with 1 tablespoon honey, remaining egg yolks and ground almonds. Fill pastry shell and arrange apple slices on top. Bake for 40 minutes. Beat remaining honey and brush it over the warm tart.

Brushing the tart with the honey while it is still warm gives it a wonderful rich glaze. You can use a honey glaze on other fruit tarts or fruit cakes.

SEPTEMBER

22

Sliced red cabbage steamed with sliced apples is a good accompaniment for rich dishes such as beef or goose.

26

23

27

24

Choose a tasty but light appetizer – such as deep-fried mushrooms in breadcrumbs or fresh tomato soup – before a strongly flavored meal.

28

25

To make Sauerkraut and Potatoes, boil 1 pound sliced potatoes until tender; do not drain. Fry 2 sliced onions and 4 ounces chopped Canadian bacon in 2 tablespoons oil and add to the potatoes with 1 pound sauerkraut. Season and thicken with 1 tablespoon cornstarch. Simmer for 30 minutes until thick.

German Pepper Steak

4 sirloin or rump steaks,
    4 ounces each
2 cloves garlic, crushed
Salt and pepper
2 tablespoons vegetable oil
2 shallots, finely chopped
4 tablespoons capers
1 cup sliced mushrooms
2 tablespoons flour
1¼ cups beef stock
1 tablespoon Dijon mustard
2 teaspoons Worcestershire
    sauce
½ cup dry white wine
2 teaspoons lemon juice
Pinch of dried thyme
Pinch of dried rosemary
8 ears baby corn
1 green pepper, sliced
1 red pepper, sliced
2 chili peppers, seeded and
    cut in half
4 ripe tomatoes, peeled
    and sliced

This is an unusual and tasty recipe that goes well with boiled rice or fried potatoes. You can substitute canned pimiento for the fresh red peppers if you prefer, and sliced dill pickles can be added with the tomatoes.

Germans often drink beer with meals instead of wine, so try serving this with a glass of chilled German lager.

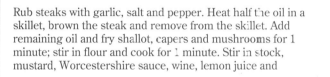

Rub steaks with garlic, salt and pepper. Heat half the oil in a skillet, brown the steak and remove from the skillet. Add remaining oil and fry shallot, capers and mushrooms for 1 minute; stir in flour and cook for 1 minute. Stir in stock, mustard, Worcestershire sauce, wine, lemon juice and herbs; bring to a boil. Add corn and peppers and return steaks to skillet. Cook for 5 minutes or until done to taste; transfer steaks to a warm serving plate. Add chili peppers and tomatoes to skillet, reheat, and spoon sauce over steaks to serve.

29

30

Simmer peeled chestnuts in chicken stock for 30 minutes until tender. Remove the chestnuts, season the sauce with salt and cayenne pepper and boil to reduce by half before pouring over the chestnuts.

September is the month for purple plums. To make Damson Chutney put 3 pounds pitted purple plums, 1 pound cored and minced apples, 3 chopped onions, 1 pound golden raisins, 2 pounds dark brown sugar, 5 cups vinegar, 2 tablespoons salt, 2 teaspoons ground sugar, 2 teaspoons ground cinnamon and 1 teaspoon allspice in a Dutch oven. Boil for about 3 hours until thick, stirring frequently. Pour into warm jars, seal, label, and store in a cool dry place.

To make Damson Preserves, place 6 pounds pitted purple plums in a Dutch oven with 2½ cups water. Bring to a boil and simmer until pulpy. Stir in 6 pounds sugar and boil rapidly for about 5 minutes to setting point.

To test whether the jam will jell, put a spoonful of jam on a cold saucer. If the jam wrinkles when pressed, it is ready. If not, boil for 4 minutes and test again.

Deviled Chicken

4 small young chickens
1 teaspoon paprika
1 teaspoon dry mustard
½ teaspoon ground turmeric
Pinch of ground allspice
4 tablespoons butter, melted
2 tablespoons chili sauce
4 sprigs watercress
1 tablespoon plum chutney

1 tablespoon steak sauce
1 tablespoon Worcestershire
sauce
1 tablespoon soy sauce
Dash of Tabasco sauce
3 tablespoons chicken stock

Tie legs of each chicken together and tuck them under the wing tips. Mix together the 5 spices, rub them all over the chickens and refrigerate for at least 1 hour. Heat oven to 350° F. Arrange chickens in a roasting pan and brush with butter. Cook for 20 minutes, basting occasionally. Mix together all remaining ingredients except watercress and brush half the mixture over the chickens. Cook for another 40 minutes, brushing with remaining sauce so skins become brown and crisp. Serve garnished with watercress.

Pasta shells go well with this dish. To cook pasta, bring a saucepan of salted water with 1 tablespoon oil to a boil, add pasta and stir. Return to a boil and cook until just tender but still slightly firm – *al dente*. Drain well and toss with butter.

October

*"O hushed October morning mild,
Thy leaves have ripened to the fall."*
Robert Frost

As THE leaves turn and the
days grow shorter and colder, the yellow, gold, red and
rust colors of the season decorate town and country. The
nights are noticeably longer, and life moves indoors.
Food takes on a more substantial form – delicious aromas
of roasting birds and baking desserts pervade the house,
creating a sense of welcome. Fall offers its last hurrah
when the sun shines on a golden October day.

OCTOBER

1

5

Make garlic croutons to serve with soup by frying cubes of bread in olive oil with 2 crushed garlic cloves.

2

If you have to keep mussels overnight, wrap them in damp newspaper and keep in the tray at the bottom of the refrigerator.

6

3

7

4

Large Dublin prawns or langoustines – as well as the giant shrimp from India – can be used for spectacular flavor and visual impact. Dublin prawns are actually a small lobster and are served in restaurants as scampi. All of these varieties are available fresh or frozen throughout the year.

Provençale Fish

1 onion, chopped
2 cloves garlic, crushed
3 tablespoons olive oil
8 medium tomatoes, peeled
   and chopped
2½ cups dry red wine
2 tablespoons tomato paste

Salt and pepper
2 pounds mussels, scrubbed
   and bearded
8 large shrimp
4 ounces peeled shrimp
4 crab claws, shelled

Fry onion and garlic gently in oil for 5 minutes until soft but
not brown. Add tomatoes and fry until just soft. Stir in wine
and tomato paste, seasoning and bring to a boil. Cover and
simmer for 15 minutes. Add mussels, cover and simmer for 5
minutes until all the mussels have opened. Discard any that
do not open. Stir in remaining ingredients and cook,
uncovered, for 8 minutes until heated through

You can buy crab claws fresh
or frozen. Crack the shell
very carefully with a
hammer or nutcracker and
remove the flesh in one
piece, retaining the
shape of the claws.

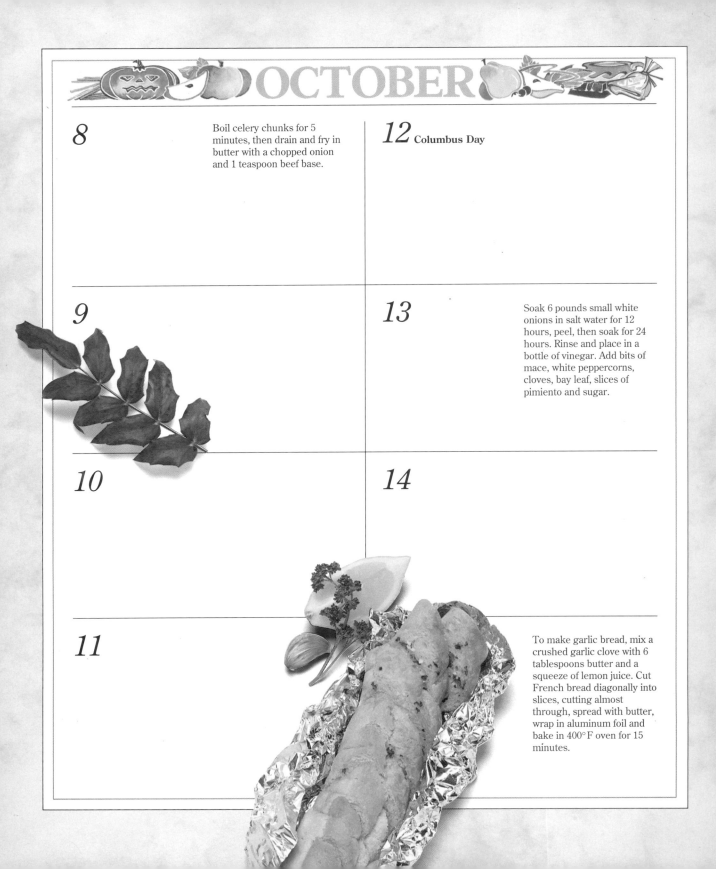

OCTOBER

8

Boil celery chunks for 5 minutes, then drain and fry in butter with a chopped onion and 1 teaspoon beef base.

12 **Columbus Day**

9

13

Soak 6 pounds small white onions in salt water for 12 hours, peel, then soak for 24 hours. Rinse and place in a bottle of vinegar. Add bits of mace, white peppercorns, cloves, bay leaf, slices of pimiento and sugar.

10

14

11

To make garlic bread, mix a crushed garlic clove with 6 tablespoons butter and a squeeze of lemon juice. Cut French bread diagonally into slices, cutting almost through, spread with butter, wrap in aluminum foil and bake in 400°F oven for 15 minutes.

Baked Spaghetti

8 ounces whole-wheat
  spaghetti, cooked
3½ cups canned tomatoes,
  chopped
1 onion, chopped
1 teaspoon dried oregano

Salt and pepper
1⅓ cups Cheddar cheese,
  grated
3 tablespoons Parmesan
  cheese, grated

Heat oven to 350° F. Grease 4 individual ovenproof dishes and
divide spaghetti between them. Spoon on tomatoes, onion
and oregano and season well with salt and pepper. Sprinkle
with Cheddar and Parmesan. Bake for 30 minutes.

Any kind of long or ribbon
pasta is suitable for this dish
– spaghetti, tagliatelli and
vermicelli are the favorites –
fresh or dried, white, green
or whole-wheat.

Cook pasta in boiling salted
water with a dash of olive oil
to prevent the pieces from
sticking together.

15

16

Peel apples as thinly as possible. It is easiest to core them with a round corer, but you can use a sharp knife.

17

18

19

20

Bake puff pastry triangles and lightly fry apple slices in butter. Slice the cooked pastry and sandwich with the apples and plain yogurt.

21

For a special dessert, peel 4 pears and scoop out cores from base. Stuff each with 1 tablespoon chopped walnuts and 4 candied cherries. Melt 4 ounces chocolate, 2 tablespoons black coffee, 2 tablespoons butter and 1 tablespoon rum. Beat in 2 egg yolks, then 2 whisked egg whites. Spoon over pears and chill.

Apples in Overcoats

1⅓ cups flour
Pinch of salt
Pinch of ground cinnamon
Pinch of freshly grated
   nutmeg
½ cup butter
4 tablespoons ice water

4 dessert apples
4 pitted prunes, chopped
4 dried apricots, chopped
1 tablespoon raisins
1 egg, beaten
6 sprigs fresh mint
1¼ cups light cream

Heat oven to 350° F. Mix flour, salt, cinnamon and nutmeg. Add butter and enough water to make a smooth dough. Divide into 4 portions; roll out and cut into 8-inch squares. Peel apples and remove cores with an apple corer. Mix together prunes, apricots and raisins. Place one apple in the center of each pastry square and fill centers with fruit mixture. Brush the edges of each square with water and fold them up around the sides of the apples. Seal them with water and trim excess pastry to give a neat finish. Roll out the pastry trimmings, cut into decorative leaves and attach to the apples. Brush with egg and bake for 25 minutes until golden brown. Garnish with mint and serve hot with cream.

Use this pastry for any sweet dishes. For extra rich pastry, use 1 egg yolk and reduce the amount of water.

Macintosh apples are especially good for this dish since they have a natural sweetness and cook well. Firm pears can also be used for this recipe and you can stuff them with any mixture of dried fruits.

OCTOBER

22

Serve winter dishes with a strong red wine such as Rioja, roasted potatoes and a selection of fresh winter vegetables.

23

24

25

26

27

Purée 1 cup cooked chick peas with 1 chopped fried onion, some parsley and 1 egg. Form into patties and fry until golden.

28

Pheasant is in season from October to January and you can buy it ready for cooking. Oven-ready frozen pheasants are available throughout the year. A hen pheasant is usually considered the tastiest and will serve three to four people; a cock pheasant is slightly larger.

Pheasant in Red Wine

1 tablespoon vegetable oil
1 tablespoon butter
1 large pheasant
2 eating apples, halved and cored
1 onion, chopped
1 tablespoon flour
⅔ cup stock or water
⅔ cup dry red wine
Juice and finely pared peel of 1 orange
2 teaspoons brown sugar
Salt and pepper
1 bay leaf
1 sprig fresh parsley
1 sprig fresh thyme

Heat oven to 350°F. Heat oil and butter and brown pheasant all over; transfer it to a casserole dish with the apples. Fry onion in the pan until soft; stir in the flour and cook for 1 minute. Stir in stock or water and wine, bring to a boil, stirring, then add the orange peel, juice and sugar. Season with salt and pepper and pour sauce over pheasant. Tie bay leaf, parsley and thyme together with string and place in casserole. Cover and bake for 1 hour until tender.

Bouquet garni is made with a selection of fresh herbs of your choice, and using the freshest herbs will give the casserole a wonderful flavor. If you do not have fresh herbs, use a bag of bouquet garni. Remember to remove the bouquet garni before serving.

29

31 Halloween

30

Shake together a dash of orange bitters, 1 tablespoon each fresh orange juice, red vermouth, white vermouth, Grand Marnier and dry gin for a Halloween Cocktail.

You can use your pumpkin shell as a Halloween lantern as well as an unusual soup bowl. Prepare the shell as described in the recipe, then draw some eyes and a mouth on one side. Cut them out carefully with a sharp knife. Cut a hole in the lid and tie some string to each side of the shell to make a handle. Put a night light in the base of the lantern and replace the lid.

Pumpkin Soup

3-pound pumpkin
4 tablespoons butter
1 large onion, sliced
1 quart water
1 cup heavy cream

Pinch of freshly grated
nutmeg
Salt and white pepper
1 tablespoon snipped
fresh chives

Wash the pumpkin well and cut around the outside of the
stem about 2 inches away from it. Carefully cut most of the
pulp off the top and set lid aside. Remove and discard the
seeds. Use a spoon to scoop out all but ½ inch of pulp from
inside without piercing the outer skin. Chop the pumpkin
pulp. Melt butter and fry onion gently for 5 minutes until
soft but not brown. Add the pumpkin and water, bring to a
boil, cover and simmer gently for 20 minutes. Purée, return
to pan and add cream, nutmeg and seasoning. Reheat and
pour into pumpkin shell.
Garnish with snipped chives.

Use a metal spoon to scoop
out and discard the stringy
pulp and seeds. Carefully
remove the pulp with a
spoon or small knife to
make a shell.

November

*"November's sky is chill and drear,
November's leaf is red and sear."*

Sir Walter Scott

ALTHOUGH the sky can be cold and gray and the trees have lost their beautiful foliage, the warmth of the kitchen can offer delights to keep the cold at bay. Nothing is as comforting as a rich soup made from fresh vegetables, sweetened with carrots and parsnips and thickened with barley – welcome nourishment for football fans who have cheered on the team in the teeth of a sharp wind. Nothing is more of a treat than the tasty pies, cakes and other desserts that provide the perfect finishing touch to a Thanksgiving feast.

NOVEMBER

1

2

3 Whisk hot cocoa in a blender until frothy and serve in a tall mug – sprinkle with chocolate shavings.

4 Parkin is a favorite English wintertime cake. Mix together ⅔ cup self-rising flour, 1⅓ cups oatmeal, ½ cup brown sugar, ½ cup dark molasses, 4 tablespoons butter, 1 egg, 5 tablespoons milk and 2 teaspoons ground ginger. Pour into a greased baking pan; bake at 350° F for 45 minutes.

5

6 Scrub some large potatoes and prick the skins with a fork. Wrap them in aluminum foil and bake them in the embers of an open fire.

7

Spicy Baked Beans

1 pound dried beans
4 ounces salt pork
1 onion

1 teaspoon dry mustard
6 tablespoons dark molasses
Salt and pepper

Soak beans in water overnight. Heat oven to 300° F. Drain
beans, transfer to a saucepan and cover with fresh water.
Bring to a boil and boil for 10 minutes. Drain and reserve the
water. Place beans, pork and onion in a large, deep casserole
dish. Mix together mustard, molasses, salt and pepper with
1¼ cups of the bean water and stir into the beans. Add the
rind of the pork. Cover casserole and bake for 2 hours. Stir in
remaining liquid and cook for a further 1½ hours until beans
are tender, uncovering for the last 30 minutes. Remove and
discard onion. Remove pork, cut off and discard rind, dice
meat and return it to the dish. Season to taste.

To make caramel apples, mix
¾ cup brown sugar, 1
tablespoon butter, ¼ cup corn
syrup, 5 tablespoons water
and ½ teaspoon vinegar. Boil
to 290° F or to point where a
droplet snaps in cold water.
Put wooden sticks into 6
apples, dip in caramel mixture,
plunge in cold water and stand
on waxed paper. Wrap any
apples not eaten immediately.

NOVEMBER

8

9 Serve pancakes with a variety of bacons: try maple-flavored and Canadian bacon, or fry bacon bits until crisp and brown.

10

11

12 Twist thickly sliced bacon in a spiral around a skewer. Broil until crisp and remove the skewer to serve.

13

14 Serve Mulled Cider hot in mugs. Mix in a saucepan 1 quart apple cider, 4 tablespoons brown sugar and a pinch of salt, and bring to a boil. Add 4 whole cloves, 1 stick cinnamon, 4 whole allspice and a strip of orange peel. Cover and simmer 15 minutes.

Potato Pancakes

1 cup grated potatoes
1 cup mashed potatoes
1⅓ cups flour
1 teaspoon salt
1 teaspoon baking soda

4 tablespoons butter, melted
4 tablespoons milk
Salt and pepper
2 tablespoons vegetable oil

Mix grated and mashed potatoes. Mix together flour, salt and baking soda and stir into potatoes. Stir in melted butter and just enough milk to make a batter of dropping consistency. Season with salt and pepper. Heat oil on a griddle or in heavy skillet and fry spoonfuls of batter until crispy and golden on both sides.

For another version of potato pancakes, mix to a consistency of batter 2 cups grated raw potatoes, 2 chopped onions, ⅓ cup chopped Canadian bacon, 1 egg and ⅓ cup flour. Add milk if needed. Fry slowly until golden brown.

NOVEMBER

15

Simmer 1 cup soaked split peas until tender, drain and mix with 1 chopped fried onion, 1 egg, salt and pepper. Bake in 350°F oven for 30 minutes.

19

16

20

17

Cook snowpeas and green beans just until tender to maintain their flavor and wonderful crisp texture.

21

18

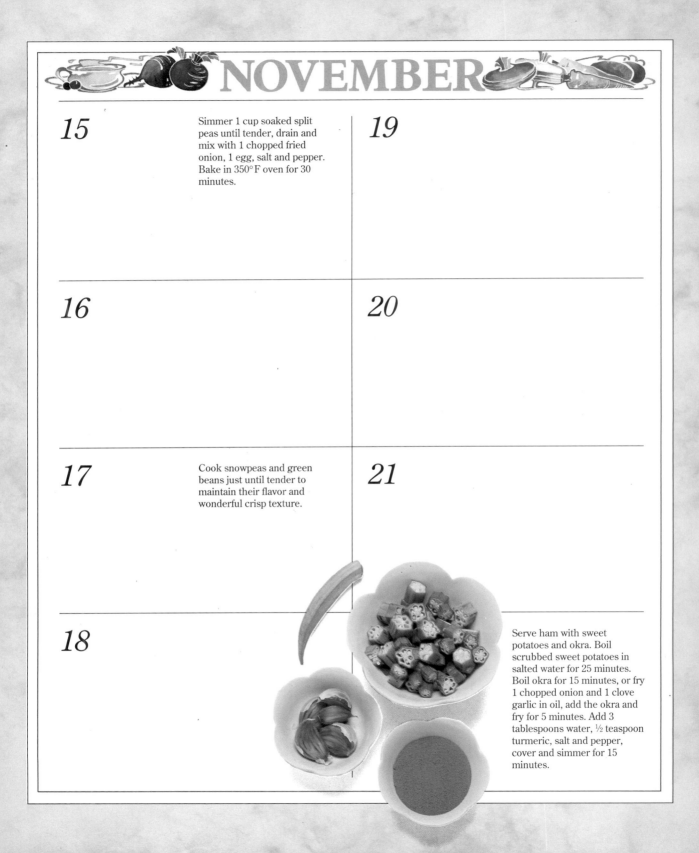

Serve ham with sweet potatoes and okra. Boil scrubbed sweet potatoes in salted water for 25 minutes. Boil okra for 15 minutes, or fry 1 chopped onion and 1 clove garlic in oil, add the okra and fry for 5 minutes. Add 3 tablespoons water, ½ teaspoon turmeric, salt and pepper, cover and simmer for 15 minutes.

Use a small sharp knife to remove the rind from the ham, leaving the fat as smooth as possible. Cut diagonal gashes in diamond shapes and stud with whole cloves for extra flavor and to give an attractive appearance.

You can use ½ cup honey instead of cola or you can boil the ham for the first half of the cooking time.

Cola Glazed Ham

10-pound smoked ham
5 cups cola

1 cup dark brown sugar
Whole cloves

Cover ham with cold water and soak overnight. Heat oven to 350° F. Set aside 3 tablespoons of cola. Place ham rind side down in a roasting pan, pour on remaining cola and bake for 2½ hours; baste frequently. Remove ham from oven and allow to cool for 15 minutes. Remove rind, leaving a ¼-inch thickness of fat. Cut diamond shapes in the fat side and insert cloves in the center of every other diamond. Mix sugar and 3 tablespoons cola; spoon over ham.

NOVEMBER

22

23

24

Brighten a Thanksgiving table with carrots and beets. Always select beets with fresh-looking leaves – one pound serves 3 or 4.

25

Carrot flowers make a colorful garnish. Peel a carrot and cut into 2-inch pieces. Cut v-shapes lengthwise down the carrot and remove the strips. Cut the carrot into thin slices. Arrange to resemble flowers, using caviar or a whole clove for the centers, chive stems and cucumber skin leaves.

26

27

Fry 3 sliced zucchini and 1 bunch sliced green onions in 1 tablespoon each sunflower and sesame oil and sprinkle with sesame seeds.

28

Zucchini and Carrot Loaf

1 onion, chopped
3 cups chopped zucchini
1 tablespoon vegetable oil
4 ounces ground almonds
⅓ cup whole-wheat bread
    crumbs
1 vegetable boullion cube,
    crushed
1 egg, beaten

1 teaspoon mixed herbs
1 tablespoon tomato paste
1 tablespoon soy sauce
Pepper
2 cups cooked, mashed carrots
1 sprig fresh rosemary
2 sprigs fresh parsley
1 carrot, cut into strips

Heat oven to 350°F. Fry onion and zucchini in oil for 5
minutes until soft. Add remaining ingredients except carrots,
rosemary and parsley; mix together well. Place half the
zucchini mixture in a greased loaf pan and press down well.
Arrange mashed carrots on top and cover with remaining
zucchini mixture. Cover with aluminum foil and bake for
1 hour. Allow to cool for 10 minutes before
removing from the pan. Garnish with
rosemary, parsley and carrot.

Rosemary is a highly
aromatic herb that goes
well with both vegetable and
meat dishes, although it
should be used in
moderation. It is a
perennial herb
that originated
in southern
Europe but
grows well in
American
gardens.

29

30

Cranberries aren't only for Thanksgiving – use extra berries to make Spiced Cranberry Preserves for Christmas. Put 1 pound cranberries and 1¼ cups cider vinegar in a large saucepan. Tie together in a cheesecloth ½-inch slice ginger root, ½-inch piece stick cinnamon and 1 teaspoon allspice berries; drop into pan. Bring to a boil and simmer for 25 minutes until the cranberries are soft and the skins pop. Stir in 1 cup sugar and simmer for 20 minutes. Remove spices and spoon mixture into warm jars.

Carrots are plentiful now, so try a tasty Carrot Cake. Cream 1 cup each butter and brown sugar. Beat in 4 egg yolks, grated peel of ½ orange and 3 teaspoons lemon juice. Stir in 1 cup self-rising flour, 1 teaspoon baking powder, 2 ounces ground almonds, 4 ounces chopped walnuts and 2 cups grated carrots. Fold in 4 whisked egg whites and spoon into a greased and floured 9-inch cake pan. Bake in a preheated 350° F oven for 1½ hours. Beat together 8 ounces cream cheese with 2 teaspoons honey and 1 teaspoon lemon juice. Spread over cooled cake and sprinkle with chopped walnuts.

Almond Lattice

6 ounces frozen puff pastry
½ cup butter
½ cup sugar
2 eggs
1 teaspoon baking powder

½ teaspoon almond extract
1 tablespoon milk
⅔ cup plain flour
4 tablespoons plum jam
2 ounces marzipan, grated

Heat oven to 400° F. Use two-thirds of the pastry to line a 10-inch quiche pan. Trim overlapping edge of pastry 1 inch from rim of pan. Cream together butter and sugar. Beat in eggs one at a time. Add almond extract and milk alternately with flour. Spread jam into pastry shell and sprinkle with marzipan. Cover with the flour and egg mixture. Make a lattice top with pastry strips. Dampen and crimp edges, folding overlapping pastry inward to form a rim. Bake for 20 minutes at 400° F; reduce heat to 350° F and bake for 15 minutes or until golden brown.

This makes a large pie, but you can reduce the quantities or make two smaller pies and freeze one. Almonds impart a distinctive flavor to this recipe. If you like a crunchier topping, sprinkle with slivered almonds before putting on the pastry lattice.

December

*"Christmas is coming, the geese are getting fat
Please to put a penny in the old man's hat."*

Anonymous

N O ONE needs to be
reminded that the holiday season is filled with joyous
events. Excitement mounts day by day, and then –
Christmas Day is here. All the planning, preparation and
work has been worthwhile. So many Christmastime
activites revolve around the kitchen, where succulent
ham, turkey, duck and a host of other treats are prepared
and brought to the table steaming hot.

DECEMBER

1

2

Fresh parsley will keep well if stored in a glass of water or in a sealed container at the bottom of the refrigerator.

3

4

5

For a tasty alternative, winter stews can be topped with flattened balls of scone dough *(August 15)* for the final 20 minutes of cooking.

6

7

To make Irish Soda Bread, mix 1⅓ cups white flour, 2⅔ cups whole-wheat flour, 2 teaspoons each cream of tartar and baking soda, 1 teaspoon each salt and sugar, 2 cups milk and 1 tablespoon yogurt. Knead into a round loaf and cut a cross on top. Bake in 400°F oven for 40 minutes.

This is an ideal recipe for making use of your crockpot, especially if you are out at work all day.

Irish Stew

2 pounds stewing lamb or
* mutton*
2 pounds potatoes, sliced
3 onions, sliced
Salt and pepper
2 tablespoons chopped fresh parsley
1 teaspoon chopped fresh thyme
1⅔ cups water

Heat oven to 275° F. Trim meat, leaving a little of the fat. Season meat and vegetables with salt, pepper, 2 teaspoons of parsley and the thyme. Layer potatoes, meat and onions in a large casserole, starting and finishing with a layer of potatoes. Add water and cover tightly. Cook for 2½ hours, shaking occasionally to prevent sticking. Check periodically to see that liquid has not cooked away; add water if needed. The potatoes will thicken the finished stew so it should not be too runny. Brown top under a hot broiler and sprinkle with remaining parsley.

Slice potatoes very thinly for this dish. You will get the best results if you use a slicer or a food processor, but a sharp knife will be fine if you make sure you slice thinly.

DECEMBER

8

England's favorite holiday dessert, immortalized in Charles Dickens' *A Christmas Carol,* has delighted British food lovers since the Middle Ages, when it was often served with meats as a first-course "porridge."

12

9

13

For sweet white sauce cook 2 ounces butter and 2 teaspoons cornstarch for 1 minute. Beat in 1 teaspoon sugar and 1 cup milk, and cook for 3 minutes.

10

14

11

Brandy or Rum Butter is delicious with plum pudding. Cream ½ cup butter until soft, then beat in ½ cup sugar, the grated peel of ½ orange and 3 tablespoons brandy or rum. Chill in small bowls and serve with the pudding.

English Plum Pudding

⅔ cup whole-wheat flour
½ pound ground suet
1⅓ cups raisins
⅔ cup golden raisins
4 ounces candied fruit peel
1 ounce chopped almonds

Grated peel of 1 lemon
½ teaspoon grated nutmeg
2 eggs, beaten
2 tablespoons honey
⅔ cup milk

Mix flour, suet, raisins, golden raisins, candied fruit peel, almonds, lemon peel and nutmeg. Whisk together eggs and honey; stir into flour-fruit mixture. Mix in milk. Pour into a greased 4-cup mold; cover with aluminum foil. Place mold in a saucepan containing about 2 inches of water. Cover and boil over low heat until wooden pick inserted in center comes out clean – about 3 hours. Add boiling water, if needed. Store in a cool dry place.
Steam for 1½ hours to heat through before serving.

Made with vegetarian suet, this is perfect for all your Christmas guests, served with a glass of sweet dessert wine.

DECEMBER

15

16

17

Make festive garnishes for cookies or cake with colored marzipan cut into stars, holly or ivy leaves, Christmas trees and Santas.

18

19

As a contrast to rich, traditional dishes, serve broiled mackerel with mashed potatoes.

20

21

Make vegetable bundles as an attractive garnish. Trim carrots, zucchini, cucumbers, peppers or celery into sticks 2 inches long and about ⅛ inch wide. Soften strips of green onions in boiling water and use them to tie up the bundles.

Spiced Beef

6 pounds rump roast
3 bay leaves, finely chopped
1 teaspoon ground mace
1 teaspoon ground cloves
1 teaspoon crushed black
   peppercorns

1 large clove garlic, crushed
1 teaspoon salt
1 teaspoon ground allspice
2 tablespoons molasses
3 tablespoons brown sugar
1 pound salt

Place beef in a large dish. Mix together all other ingredients; rub into meat. Cover and refrigerate for 24 hours. Repeat process every day for a week, turning the meat and rubbing in the spices; these will blend with the juices drawn from the meat. Tie the meat up firmly and place in a saucepan. Cover with water and simmer gently for 6 hours. Allow to cool in saucepan with liquid. Transfer to a serving dish; slice very thinly to serve.

It takes time for the meat to absorb the spices and flavorings that tenderize it while imparting their wonderful tastes.

Served cold and thinly sliced, this is a great Christmas dish. It takes a little time, but is not difficult to prepare.

22

Brush squares of phyllo dough with melted butter, fill with mincemeat and twist the tops to seal. Bake in 400°F oven for 10 minutes.

24 Christmas Eve

23

25 Christmas Day

Children can make cutlet frills. Fold an 8x6-inch piece of paper in half lengthwise, making a long, soft fold. Make narrow cuts into the fold to within ¾ inch of the edge. Wind the paper around your finger and fix with glue or tape.

To make Sausage Stuffing, heat 4 tablespoons oil in a skillet and brown 4 ounces bulk sausage. Add 3 diced stalks celery, 2 chopped onions, 4 ounces walnuts and ⅔ cup raisins. Cook for 5 minutes, stirring constantly. Remove from heat and drain off fat. Mix in 1 loaf day-old bread, cubed. Add 1¼ cups chicken stock, 2 tablespoons chopped fresh parsley, and a pinch each of thyme, sage, salt and pepper; mix well.

An Apricot and Apple Stuffing goes well with the fattier meat of goose or duck at Christmas. Cook, drain and chop 12 ounces dried apricots and put juice aside. Mix the apricots with 1 tablespoon brown sugar, 1 chopped green pepper, 1 chopped cooking apple, 4 chopped stalks celery, ½ cup bread crumbs, ⅓ cup melted butter, grated peel of 1 orange, 2 eggs, salt and pepper. Bind with 5 tablespoons apricot juice.

Holiday Turkey

16-pound turkey   *6 tablespoons butter*

Heat oven to 325°F. Fill neck cavity of turkey with sausage stuffing; do not pack – stuffing will expand while cooking. Place remaining stuffing in small greased casserole dish and cover. Tie turkey legs together; do not cross legs. Tuck neck skin under wing tips and fasten with skewers. Place turkey, breast side up, on rack in shallow roasting pan and spread butter over breast and legs. Cover loosely with aluminum foil tent and cook for 2½ hours, basting frequently. Remove foil and roast for 2 to 2½ hours more until juices run clear when the thickest part of the thigh is pierced with a skewer. Cook extra stuffing for last 45 minutes of cooking time. Cover turkey and let stand 20 minutes before carving. Remove all stuffing from turkey. After serving, cool stuffing and turkey meat promptly; refrigerate separately. Use stuffing within 1 or 2 days and turkey meat within 2 or 3 days. Turkey meat can be frozen up to 3 weeks.

DECEMBER

26

27
Fry slices of leftover plum pudding in butter, dust with sugar and serve with ⅔ cup heavy cream whipped with 1 tablespoon powdered sugar and 2 tablespoons port wine.

28

29

30

31 New Year's Eve

To make Champagne Cocktail, drop a lump of sugar into a champagne flute and soak it with Angostura bitters. Add two dashes of brandy and top with chilled Champagne. Garnish with a slice of orange and a cherry.

Spiced Nut Cake

1⅓ cups flour
1 teaspoon baking powder
1 cup sugar
Pinch of salt
Pinch of freshly grated
   nutmeg
Pinch of ground ginger

½ cup orange juice
2 tablespoons butter, melted
4 tablespoons water
1 egg, beaten
⅔ cup cranberries
4 ounces hazelnuts, chopped
1 tablespoon powdered sugar

You can replace the hazelnuts with chopped walnuts or almonds, and use candied cherries and candied fruit peel instead of cranberries.

Heat oven to 325°F. Grease and line a 9x5-inch loaf pan. Sift dry ingredients together in a mixing bowl and make a hole in center. Stir in the orange juice, butter, water and egg. Beat well; stir in cranberries and nuts. Spoon mixture into loaf pan and bake for 1 hour or until wooden pick inserted in center comes out clean. Remove from pan and dust with powdered sugar. Slice and serve warm or cold with butter or cream cheese.

Index of Recipes

Dates refer to the first date on each left-hand page.